Dedicated
to animal lovers
everywhere

Acknowledgments

The photo on the back cover was shot by Mona Doerre
of Mona Doerre Photography:
www.monadoerre.de
https://www.instagram.com/monadoerrephotography/

Many thanks to Beverly Haney,
owner of UniGraphics for her beautiful cover design
and book layout. For more information about Beverly,
contact her at beverly.haney@att.net.

Lastly, much appreciation to my amazing editor,
Victoria Mack. For more information about Victoria,
contact her at vicsidhan@gmail.com.

Foreword

"Clearly, animals know more than we think, and think a great deal more than we know."

This quote by Irene M. Pepperberg, a notable scientist in the field of animal cognition, speaks to my soul.

As an animal communicator, I firmly believe that the animals we share our world with have much to teach us. *And* I believe that their emotions and souls are deeper and more complex than we could ever imagine.

Sadly, for now, many are waiting.

Waiting for the human race to wake up. Waiting for us to be their voice. Waiting for us to stop abusing them. And waiting for us to start learning from their example. But for some, the waiting game *is* over. And they have found their perfect relationships.

The stories in this book celebrate the magical connection between humans and their four-legged heroes. It illustrates what our animal companions teach us, the advice our animals would give us if we took the time to ask, and the special partnership between people and their beloved animal companions as they help each other navigate their life path.

As an author and animal communicator, I am honored to be the teller of these stories.

Barney and Mike

"This is bringing back memories I haven't revisited for thirty years," Mike said, clearing his throat and pausing to regain his composure. "I'd forgotten how special this dog was and how much he added to my life."

I met Mike through a mutual friend. I was looking for an editor for my first book, and my friend suggested I contact Mike. After we finished my first book, he shared Barney's story with me.

Before Barney, Mike had never had a dog…or any animal companion for that matter. He'd spent his childhood in a cramped Bronx apartment barely suitable for a cat or small dog. A large dog would have been out of the question.

Later, in his twenties, Mike lived in Ohio and sold fish tanks, dog bones, and pet supplies to stores. During his rounds one day, he entered a shop in Indianapolis. Along one wall, several crates housed dogs. Two German Shepherds, a black Lab, and a litter of German Shepherd puppies. As he strolled past each crate, the adult dogs rose and barked excitedly and wagged their tails furiously, hoping to attract his attention.

When he reached the crate with the puppies, each yipped and jumped as if to say, "Choose me! Choose me!" Except for one. A small, unassuming, black-and-tan male, arguably the runt of the litter. Mucus drained from his nose and eyes, and he sat quietly while his littermates yapped. Then he looked at Mike and wagged his tail feebly twice. The deal was sealed.

"I've never believed in love at first sight," Mike said. "But that's what happened when I saw Barney. Our eyes met, and I think we both knew it was meant to be."

Mike told me he had been toying with the idea of getting a dog, but he wasn't actively looking. His connection with Barney was fated. And he called his wife and told her he was bringing home a new friend.

When Barney recovered from his cold, he became a loving, playful puppy. And he discovered his voice, yowling to Mike and vocalizing what he couldn't say in human words.

"I wish I'd known what he was saying," Mike said. "If I'd known you then," he said with a chuckle, "I could have just asked you."

Looking back, he admitted, he really hadn't a clue about what having a dog would mean. He knew nothing about training, socialization, or interpreting the physical and verbal cues. Nor was he knowledgeable about nutrition or the emotional and physical needs of a puppy. So he took classes and read books, but housetraining, especially, eluded him. Barney had frequent accidents, which were a source of frustration, but ultimately Mike didn't care. He only knew that he loved Barney.

Mike and his wife lived in a tiny duplex, and though they had a small yard, it wasn't fenced. During the day, Barney spent a few hours in the backyard on a long tether that allowed him to roam and play on the grass. School kids cut through their yard in the mornings, and Barney greeted each with affection, letting them pet him or flopping on his back for a belly scratch.

"When I remember this," Mike admits, "I roll my eyes and realize how naïve we were. I'd *never* have a dog tethered in the backyard now. Now, my dogs are like my children. I'd do anything for them."

"We all make mistakes with our animal companions," I said. "I certainly did. Even the most well-intentioned pet parents do. Like you, the best ones learn from their blunders and apply the lessons to their next companions."

A year later, Mike, his wife, and Barney moved to Southern California. Mike's wife was a nurse and often worked long hours. Mike bought a bookstore and worked days. Often, he and Barney would fill their spare time on the weekends taking long walks and hiking the grassy, rural foothills for hours. There, in the peace and solitude of those open fields, Barney could run free. They created a ritual that would become Barney's favorite pastime. Mike tossed ball after ball in the air, striking it with a bat and launching the ball yards into the distance. Barney barreled after each ball, retrieving dozens until he tired and lay down in front of Mike, indicating that he was done.

Three years after their move, Mike's bookstore went out of business. The stress of what he considered to be a failure ate away at him, causing an ulcer that almost took his life. When he recovered, he turned to his true love, writing, and years later became an award-winning author.

"I decided to follow my dream and write rather than sell books," he said, "and it allowed me to work from home and spend more time with Barney."

When Barney turned five, Mike and his wife had their first child. Worried that the dog would be territorial or aggressive, Mike's wife wanted to put Barney down. Mike intervened.

"It was crazy to even think about," he said. "And there was no way I was going along with that. He was my friend. He *was* my first child. Once the baby came, I just made sure things were never out of hand. And they never were. Barney adjusted, and by the time we had two more children, Barney was a pro at babysitting."

Eventually, the years took their toll on Mike and his wife, and their marriage was on the rocks. But because of his upbringing, divorce wasn't even on his radar. The stress and toxicity of his relationship ate at him. He was often tired and appeared aged beyond his years. Although his health suffered, his connection with Barney was a constant positive that he clung to.

"I was miserable," Mike said, reflecting on his marriage, "but Barney got me through it. Looking back, I realize that I wasn't even in touch with how depressed I'd become. My only positive connection beyond my children was my relationship with Barney. He was my salvation."

As Mike's health declined, so did Barney's. He no longer had the energy to chase the ball. Even walking short distances tired him. Then quite suddenly, Barney's health deteriorated further. One evening, Mike lounged on the sofa with Barney at his feet. Barney rose to get some water, but his legs shook and his body trembled. Then he collapsed. Mike rushed to him and called the vet, a family friend, who raced to Mike's home. Barney died in Mike's arms just minutes after he had placed the call.

Tormented by the loss of his dog, Mike pulled inward. Night after night, he dreamt about Barney. His marriage deteriorated even further, and Mike and his wife divorced soon after Barney's death.

Years later, alone in his apartment, Mike lay sprawled on the sofa, fading in and out of sleep. Jazz tunes played softly in the background. Suddenly, he had a vision of Barney. His beloved friend stood near, and his familiar doggy scent filled the room. Barney put his paw on Mike's arm. Then the vision disappeared.

"I wondered if I was dreaming," Mike said. "But I could hear the jazz music in the background. And I could smell him. When he put his paw on my arm, it was as though he was telling me, 'I'm OK, Dad. I'm OK. It's OK to let me go.'"

Mike released his emotion in regard to Barney's death by writing him into two of his books. In the first, a special dog has an emotional reunion with a human he has left behind. In the second, man and dog play ball in a grassy field one last time. It was a writer's way of seeking closure. If closure is truly possible.

While I was writing Mike's story, I tuned into Barney to ask him about his life with Mike, knowing that with the gap in the years, he could be a different being now. It was possible that he had come back to earth in another form. Or more probable, he'd reincarnated several times. But I trusted that his spirit would hold memories of his life with Mike. And if I couldn't reach him, I trusted that my guides could tap into the information I needed.

I asked him what he felt when Mike walked through the doors of the pet shop. His response came through clearly.

I was scared. So scared. My brothers and sisters weren't sick like I was. They were happy, and outgoing, and strong. I felt that they would get homes. But I worried that I would be overlooked. My greatest fear was that I would be left alone in that cage.

Then I asked him what his purpose had been with Mike. But he ignored me.

I want to thank him. I'd like to thank him.

"Thank him for what?" I asked.

For everything he did for me. He saved my life when he took me from that pet store. He saved my life. I want you to tell him that.

"Did you know he saved you after that? That his wife wanted to put you down?"

I had a sense that something wasn't right. I could feel that she had made a shift.

"I wonder, have you any advice for us? What would it be?"

Who is "us"?

"Humans. The human race."

Start learning from us. We don't distrust or dislike just because someone is different. It all stems from fear. You fear what you don't understand. When fear turns into ignorance and then hatred, it's the root of many of your problems.

I agree. It is something I wish for too. That we could be more open. More trusting. More respectful of differences. I paused and let his message sink in. "What was your purpose with him, with Mike?" I asked again.

I helped him find his true path.

"Which was…"

To find true love.

"Mmm," I said. A muffled noise rattled slightly in my chest like an internal sigh.

When I asked Mike what he thought he had learned from Barney, he responded, "Patience and love. Patience," he said, "because I was so clueless about dogs. So I was easily frustrated. Now, I realize my frustration was about my ineptness to communicate with him, not about his behavior. He taught me to approach things differently. They give so much, yet they ask for so little."

"They do do that," I said and then smiled. "And love… what did he teach you about love?"

"Well," he said, "other than Barney and my children, there wasn't much love in my life. My marriage wasn't a love relationship. Barney showed me what love could be like."

"How do you think your life would have been different if Barney hadn't been a part of it?" I asked.

"In my family, the men have a history of dying young. I worried about that happening to me. That, coupled with the stress and toxicity of my relationship, took a tremendous toll on my health. Without Barney, I wouldn't have made it. He showed me what companionship could mean. He showed me what true happiness felt like. He taught me what true love was, and once I was divorced, I knew I could have it again."

Years later, Mike met his soulmate. The woman who would become the love of his life. And they have now been together for twenty-six years. I think Barney helped Mike to believe that he was worthy of that. Deserving of that kind of love. A love that's unconditional. A love that beckons you to open your heart and blossom. A love that only a soulmate—human or canine—can give you.

Hartley and Martha

"I remember it like it was yesterday," she said. "I was sitting at my desk, head down, banging out prose on my computer, and I hear these squeals of delight from out in the hall. I walked out to investigate and saw two colleagues, Ryan and Renee, playing with the most adorable puppy I had ever seen. Part Dachshund, part Chihuahua, and just this darling little brown-and-black-spotted bundle. I'm not a dog person, but I knelt down, and he looked into my eyes, jumped right into my lap, and snuggled into me. I looked at Ryan and said, 'Whose puppy is this?'"

"Yours," he replied. "He and his brother were surrendered by a breeder. I'm trying to find homes for them."

"I sort of balked when Ryan said that. Nor was I sure what to do. But something tugged at me. At my heart. I consulted another colleague. Someone I really trusted with all big decisions. His response hit home. He said, 'Martha, whenever you have the opportunity to love or be loved unconditionally, the answer is always yes.'"

Still, Martha then had a big decision to make. She hadn't had a dog in years. She considered herself a cat person. She waged the classic head-versus-heart battle. Was she too busy? Could she make room in her life for a new family member? Yet somehow she knew this was fated. She'd known it from the moment she looked into his eyes that she'd met her canine soulmate. And in the first twenty-four hours, she didn't question her decision. After all, it was one she'd made with her heart.

The following day, reality set in. How would she make sure he was OK during the day? How would she work out? How would she see friends? She felt she couldn't leave him at home. He was just a pup. The solution? She rearranged her life around him, and Hartley went everywhere with her.

"The reality is," she laughed, "I drew the lucky card when I chose Hartley. Ryan brought two puppies that day. Brothers. Hartley's brother is a bit of a handful from what I hear. Luckily for me, Hartley and I chose each other."

Hartley came to work with her and slept in a crate. They could often be seen walking the nature path that connected the five buildings of the company she and I worked for. He became the office darling and the company his second home. Instead of going to the gym, she bought a doggie backpack and starting hiking, toting Hartley on her back. During her women's group and writers' meetings, he slept peacefully on her lap.

"What floored me was how good he was from the beginning. He didn't bark or go crazy. He never chewed things. It was like he was an old soul, not a puppy. He just seemed to sense when he needed to behave. He's really such a dignified little guy. It's as though he has an on/off button that determines how he behaves in every situation. And he always knows when he should be on and when he should be off."

Hartley is, as his name implies, all heart. A huge, loving heart encased in the tiniest body imaginable. Martha laughed and said he could tend to be jealous. Of her cat or anything that might steal attention from him. Then he nudges her or wriggles himself into the crook of her arm to remind her where her focus should be.

"He's a Scorpio," she said in explanation. "They're intense. And it's all about them."

Years before Hartley came into Martha's life, her adult son disappeared. He'd been missing for the better part of seven years. She had shared this with me over lunch one day. As a mother myself, I felt her pain. I have a son several years younger than Martha's. The thought of not knowing how he was or where he was would leave a gaping hole in my heart. The thought of being unable to help him would be unbearable. But she soldiers on. With the hope that one day they will be reconnected. In documenting her story about Hartley, I asked her about her son.

"He's still missing," she said.

"I'm so sorry. I thought you'd reunited with him. I thought he was back."

"He was. Briefly. All too briefly. That was two years ago. I haven't seen him since."

I paused for a moment and then asked, "Do you think that Hartley played a role in reconnecting you and your son in that time? Because intuitively that's what I'm sensing."

"Oh, without a doubt," she responded. "Hartley was the catalyst for my son's decision to visit me. I think Hartley brought innocence to the situation that made my son feel safe. It was the first time I'd seen him in years. He'd been homeless and wandering. Out of the blue, I got an email from him. From Chicago. I emailed back, telling him about Hartley and attaching a photo. And he responded with 'pretty cute.' But I could tell from his words that he wasn't well. He's schizophrenic. It causes him to think that people aren't real but rather possessed by alien or demonic energy. He hears voices. Horrible voices. He's very ill, and it's tragic for me. His condition is genetic. My mother and I both have some imbalances with our brain chemistry, but we're able to manage it."

She continued to tell me about when she and her son reunited. Through email, they agreed that she'd wire him money to take a bus to California. He felt that people from the government were watching him. And he was afraid to fly. On the day of his arrival, she drove to the Escondido bus depot. She brought Hartley along, and when her son got off the bus, ragged and bearded, he walked straight into her arms, hugged her and Hartley, kissed her cheek, tousled Hartley's head, and said, "I love you, Mom."

"I knew in that moment my son had clarity," she said, her voice husky with emotion. "And I knew that he still loved me. It's a gift that I'll always carry in my heart."

She brought him home and got him settled. Life on the road is tough, and although he's only in his late twenties, lack of nourishment, rest, and care had aged him. Through his emails, she knew he'd been eating from garbage cans and sleeping in tunnels. Martha dove into "mom mode," cleaning, cooking, and nurturing her beloved son. And for a while everything seemed fine.

Then he began asking strange questions about their connection. He began to doubt she was his real mom but rather a shell filled with demonic alien energy that simply looked like his mom. One day, he stormed out the door and raced down the street, screaming that he couldn't trust her. Martha ran after him, pleading with him to come back, sobbing and swearing that she'd take a blood test to prove she was really his mother. But it was too late. He'd snapped again. The voices in his head had won.

"It was like reliving a nightmare. I couldn't stop him or help him."

A friend called Martha a few days later, telling her that he'd spotted her son at a local park. Martha called 911 to request that a psychiatric emergency response team find him and talk to him. A team was dispatched, and they connected with Martha's son.

"But despite his issues," she said, "he's sane enough to know what was going on. He had all the right answers and didn't meet the criteria for being 'gravely disabled,' so they couldn't hospitalize him."

"Beyond that, why do you think Hartley is in your life?" I asked.

"So many reasons," she responded, her voice cracking. "He's my stability. Absolutely my emotional stability as I go through one of the most horrific things a mother can go through. It's an open wound."

I paused because I was crying now, imagining myself in her situation. After a moment, I placed my hand to my heart. "I'm so sorry for what you're going though, and I'm so moved you would share all this with me."

"It's good to talk about it. It helps me process." She chucked Hartley under the chin and said, "This dog is loving, grounding energy. A psychic once told me that I must always have a pet to ground me because I'm an empath. I feel everything around me. And they do stabilize me."

Like most dogs do for their people, Hartley serves many purposes for Martha. He's her rock. Her heart. He balances her. Reminds her to take breaks. Reminds her to play.

"Before Hartley," she said, "I'd work nonstop. Now he forces me to take breaks. We jog up to the little lawn on the hill behind the conference room, and we play fetch. Can you imagine me playing fetch in the middle of the day?" She laughed and said, "I'm less compulsive with him around."

When Martha first brought Hartley into her life, she wondered how things might change. Wondered if maybe her world would be altered. And it was altered, but not the way she thought. Hartley has expanded her world, not confined it. Pre-Hartley, Martha worked long hours, gave much of her life to her career, worked her body hard at the gym. Lived in a beautiful neighborhood but never had time to savor the nature trails that snaked through the surrounding area. Post-Hartley, she travels more, has more human and canine friends, laughs more, and plays more.

"He's so easy to travel with because he loves his crate. I can take him anywhere—in the car, on planes—and he's just such an ambassador. He lowers the barriers."

"I know," I said. "Dogs just invite other humans to come up and meet you. We're all far more approachable and interesting at the end of a leash."

"I've lived in this neighborhood for years," she said, "yet I never took the time to walk the trails. I'm closer to my neighbors and my community and the splendors of nature because of this little guy." She picked him up and kissed his nose. "And he has his own little pack of friends that we meet on the trails. It's so joyful to watch him run free with them. He's like a little greyhound. He just flies."

I tuned in to Hartley and asked him what it was like when he first met Martha.

His response burst through like sunshine from behind a cloud. *She's FOUND me!* he exclaimed.

"So you were meant to be together then?"

All pairings are meant to be. For whatever reason.

"What's your reason? Your purpose together?"

Love. Is there any purpose greater than that?

"No. There is no purpose greater than that." I paused for a moment and then asked my next question. "What do you do for her? How do you help her?"

I keep her focused. Which sounds strange because she is focused. I suppose it's more appropriate to say that I help her balance. Which allows her to focus and accomplish what she needs to on all levels. Dimensionally. Spiritually. It has to do with magnetics and helping her attract and translate and understand the things she brings into her being and then manifest that into the world.

"That's a big job. Big responsibility."

Somebody's got to do it.

I laughed. And realized again how powerful our animal companions are. What seems big or complex or even beyond our comprehension, they do almost without effort.

"What would you like Martha to know about you that she doesn't?"

I am an agitator of forces. I shake things up. It keeps our world moving.

"How would you describe Martha?"

She's gentle. Like a caretaker, she guards the Earth. Warm. Nurturing. It's like she wraps her arms around the planet and protects it. As though her soul lives in every mountain, stream, forest, and ocean. She's connected to the heart and soul of our planet.

It was the perfect description of her.

"How has being with her transformed your life?"

I am fully manifested. I am everything I came into this world to be.

His response touched my heart, and I teared up. For there is no more powerful experience and no greater gift than being exactly who we planned to be.

When I asked Martha why she thought she and Hartley had come to be together, she responded that he deserved it. That he deserved to be made the center of someone's world.

When I asked her what Hartley had taught her, she responded, "To learn to drop everything and love, right in the moment. There's nothing better."

Hartley is Martha's life. He's her mirror. Her joy. He was a catalyst for bringing her son home for that brief but powerful visit. And because of that, she has a sense of closure in the fact that they reconnected.

"I now know how much my son loves me," she said, "and, because of that, I have hope, and I carry that hope that there can one day be some help for him. That one day my son may be well. And I might not have had any of that without this special little dog."

Mambo and Jenny

"It was on my birthday in 2014," she said. "That was the day everything changed for me."

I was interviewing Jenny, Mambo's person, as well as her mother, Angelika. I had discovered Jenny and Mambo on YouTube several years earlier when one of their videos popped up in my queue.

In the first video I watched, Jenny, a beautiful, young blonde with golden skin and sky-blue eyes, sat astride Mambo, her stunning, coal-black Friesian stallion. His thick neck, swan-like yet sturdy, arched upward from his powerfully sloped shoulders. His dense, curly mane cascaded from his neck, wafting slightly in the spring breeze as he stood poised and alert. Then, at Jenny's cue, he exploded into a gallop, thundering across the green German countryside as she spread her arms, gracefully mimicking a bird in flight.

I continued to watch their video montage, entranced as she cued Mambo to bow in their arena, to come nibble her shoulder when she tapped it, to trot after her in a zig zag pattern, and to kiss her check when she motioned him to do so. As I watched the final portion of the video, a still shot of her holding her beloved horse's head in her arms while the sun set behind them, bathing them in a golden glow, my throat knotted and tears rolled down my cheeks. I had just witnessed their love story as it unfolded before me. And it reminded me of my deep connection to my own horse, Bear.

Jenny and Mambo are a team. The fairytale-like connection they share is rare. Like catching lightning in a bottle, they have captured the hearts of thousands through social media. He is her best friend and she his. She's a breathtakingly beautiful rider. Correct, fluid, and balanced. And Mambo is a commanding, powerful, and gorgeous boy. The Black Star is one of the nicknames she has bestowed upon him. Although he is a stallion, he is putty in her hands. But it wasn't always that way. And on the day I interviewed her, I learned more about their moving story.

Jenny first met Mambo when she was fourteen years old. Her mom had arranged for his owner to have a job at the barn where Jenny and her sisters took riding lessons, and Mambo's owner began boarding him there. Jenny was riding a tall Warmblood mare at the time. The Warmblood breeds originated from Europe, and they excel at jumping and dressage, a classic form of riding and specific agility maneuvers.

Jenny didn't fully appreciate Mambo at first because Friesians aren't generally used for dressage due their stockier builds. And dressage and Warmbloods were her passions. But after some time, the horse's regal beauty caught her eye. She began spending time with Mambo, walking him around the stable grounds to cool him off and grooming him after his owner rode. Soon their bond began to form.

After just a few weeks, her conversations with others were peppered with mentions of Mambo. And before long, she was crazy about the horse, but because she was only fourteen, she wasn't allowed to ride him. But the connection between them became so apparent that Mambo's owner acquiesced and allowed Jenny to begin to ride him several times a week, often coaching the pair as they worked.

I asked Angelika if she had any concerns about her young daughter riding such a huge and powerful horse and a stallion at that.

"A stallion, yes. Mambo, no," she replied. "He's an energetic boy for sure. But he's kind and unbelievably well-behaved. When I first met him, two years before my children did, I told the owner that owning a horse was not my dream, but if I ever did, I would want one just like Mambo."

And I would have to agree with her. As you watch his videos, the amazing thing about Mambo is that, even though he's a stallion, he rarely seems to get rattled.

One day, on a trail ride, a wild boar sprang in front of Jenny and Mambo and dashed across the road, disappearing into the brush. Jenny jumped off to console him, but he seemed only mildly interested. In another incident, after a show he seemed to not want to get into the trailer. Yet instead of panicking or pulling back, he just stopped and stood quietly. Jenny backed him up, tried three more times to load him, and was successful. Another time, Jenny had arranged to ride with a friend. It was a first meeting for both horses. Jenny walked Mambo until the two horses were nose to nose. The other horse screamed and struck at Mambo with its left front hoof. Mambo stood calmly without reacting.

And in the dozens of videos I watched to understand their back story, I've rarely seen him display the kind of behavior stallions often do when they become interested in a mare. While he conveys the classic Friesian curiosity and he's interested in what's going on around him, he is, for the most part, relatively unflappable. He is truly a once-in-a-lifetime horse.

If Mambo were human, he'd certainly have a zest for life. He's a playful boy, and Jenny often captures video of him jumping and bucking in his turnout, playfully rearing with his pasture mates, and nibbling her back while she grooms him. One of his funniest moments was a video of him appreciatively admiring himself in the mirrors that line the walls of the indoor riding arena, nuzzling his reflection and steaming the glass with his breath.

"He falls in love with himself anew each time he sees his reflection in the glass," Jenny laughed.

Jenny had been riding Mambo for three years when they had a serious accident. She galloped Mambo in a field while her friend videotaped them. Suddenly, Mambo spooked and jumped sideways, racing headlong across the meadow. The saddle girth hadn't been tightened enough, and his jarring movement caused the saddle to slip down his side. Jenny fought to regain her balance, her left leg digging into his withers, but she continued to slip down his right side as the saddle slid further.

She attempted to leap from the saddle to free herself, but her right foot caught in the stirrup, and in two more strides, she was almost under his belly, trapped in the saddle.

He leapt to the left, his feet dancing on the ground as if he were stepping on hot coals, in an attempt to free himself from her. You could see from the video footage she posted after the accident how hard he tried to avoid stepping on her. But she was directly underneath him now, and there was no avoiding what would happen next. His back hoof struck the top of her head and her face moments before her foot was freed from the stirrup. He leapt away from her and raced across the field, dragging the saddle upside down under his belly. Jenny jumped to her feet, at first unaware she was injured, and sprinted after Mambo to make sure he was unhurt. Then she saw blood gushing from her mouth and head and screamed to her friend to call an ambulance.

While Mambo was checked for wounds and ushered back to the barn, Jenny was helicoptered to the University Clinic in Frankfurt, where she remained for one week. Surgeons operated on her to repair her fractured body. Her teeth, while not broken, were loosened from the fall, so they stitched her gums and lip. Her back was injured, and her chest had been broken in four places. Titanium was placed in two of the three skull fractures to stabilize them. And she was covered in bruises. The doctors told her that, without her helmet, she wouldn't have survived. And it would be three more weeks before she would be cleared to ride again.

I asked Angelika if she had any fear of Jenny returning to riding after such a horrific accident.

"Well, it was awful, of course," she responded. "But as soon as I got to the hospital, Jenny said, 'Mum, it wasn't his fault. I didn't tighten the cinch well enough. He did everything to avoid hurting me. And I'm not going to stop riding him.' And so I trust her. She does very well with him. And I also trust him. I trust him with my daughter's life."

I asked Jenny if she had been afraid to get back to riding once she was allowed.

"No," she said. "The accident was my fault. Well," she said, pausing to reflect, "there was some fear in those first few moments when I put my toe in the stirrup. Like butterflies in my stomach. But once I was in the saddle, we were back to normal."

2013 would prove to be a pivotal year for Jenny and Mambo. Mambo's owner lost her job. And with no resources to pay for the board at the barn, she turned to a friend who had a plot of land in the forest with a lush, fenced meadow, where she could board him for free. Reluctantly, she turned Mambo loose in the meadow. Jenny and her mom visited every day, often meeting the owner there. And Jenny would ride Mambo in the forest. He was well cared for, but it broke all of their hearts when they inevitably needed to leave him at night, knowing how social and connected to them he was.

One night in October, a massive storm hit their area, bringing torrential rains and freezing winds. Mambo had been in the forest for three weeks.

"I worried about him all night," Angelika recalls. "He was without shelter, and I fretted about how he was faring. I doubt I slept for more than ten minutes. And I decided the next day that we would go get him and bring him back to the barn where Jenny and her sisters took lessons. And we would pay for his care. I contacted the owner, and she agreed. I never wanted her to repay us. But I needed to do this for Jenny and Mambo. And his owner. I didn't want his owner to lose him. She loved him as much as we did."

Jenny and her mom set out into the forest the next day with their truck and trailer. As they got out of the truck, Mambo trotted to the fence, whinnying to them and tossing his head. They haltered him and led him to the trailer, and he trotted into it.

"I've never seen him get into the trailer so fast," Jenny said. "I think he knew he was coming back to his home."

At the farm, they were greeted by friends and family holding welcome signs and cheering. A huge white banner with the word *Willkommen* stenciled in blocky, red letters hung over the barn. Tears welled in Jenny's eyes, and she looked at her mom, overwhelmed and touched, murmuring, "Aww."

For the next few months, Jenny threw herself into caring for Mambo. Spending hours riding, grooming, training, and sometimes just lying in the pasture pouring her heart out to him. But as idyllic as their life was, there would be three things that would test them.

The first, he was plagued with lameness issues for months, which meant frequent vet visits, medication, and consults with the farrier to understand the cause. Finally, it was determined that the lameness could be corrected through proper shoeing and a saddle that was custom-fitted to the shape of his back.

The second, Mambo was nine years old by then, and his age brought on what is known as the second of three phases of puberty. During this phase, the horse's stallion-like ways can escalate, and Mambo was definitely feeling his power. He began rearing and testing Jenny and becoming far too interested in other mares. And he was much harder to handle. But Jenny never let it rattle her. She simply kept her cool and worked through his behavior with patience. She will be the first to tell you that if anything goes wrong with their work, it is her responsibility. And she believes that the right way to solve their problems is to never give up, but rather to get creative.

The third, Mambo's owner was having increased financial difficulties and was seriously considering selling him. Even though she loved him. For six months, Mambo's fate hung in the balance while his owner tried to make a decision. And every day, Jenny fretted about the outcome. Was this the day she would lose her best friend? The uncertainty was overwhelming. At times, she just sat in his stall staring at him through her tears, her worry overshadowing all else.

Three months before Jenny's eighteenth birthday, her parents made the decision to buy Mambo. Only Jenny's siblings and his former owner knew. And they planned to make the momentous announcement during a show that she and Mambo would participate in on her birthday.

At the show, Jenny and Mambo placed in the ribbons. Afterward, there was a casual celebration of her birthday in the covered arena, and Jenny's sister read a poem to her that foreshadowed what was about to happen. As her sister uttered the last sentence of the speech announcing the surprise, Jenny doubled over, spilling tears of joy into her cupped, gloved hands. Thunderous applause filled the arena, and she turned to see her parents walking Mambo back into the show ring, two red bows fluttering from the sides of his halter. She hugged her sister and then ran to her parents, laughing though her tears and embracing them, her siblings, her friends, and Mambo, one by one.

A dream she'd never expected had come true. Their fate was no longer undecided. The nagging fear of losing him was put to rest. This beautiful, beloved boy, The Black Star, was hers forever.

The afternoon was documented on camera with speeches of congratulation and well wishes in a video montage that ended with Jenny sitting on Mambo, repeatedly leaning forward to wrap her arms around his neck and kiss him, whispering, "I love you. You are mine now," through her tears.

One day, she posted a poem on her Facebook wall that she'd written to him. It said simply...

Love is not an emotion or something that can be defined by the self or it would not be eternal. To embrace it one needs to surrender to it. This is because love has little to do with the self and everything to do with others. Love is as love does which is something you do not just do, it is something you feel. So love defines and is not defined. Love becomes visible to those who discover selflessness and learn to give. Love is the giving of the self in the purest form. This is how I love you.

Despite the beauty you'll see in Jenny's videos, her days are sometimes anything but glamorous. She works full-time for an organization where her mom, dad, and sister also work so that she can pay for Mambo's board and care. And she spends her off hours cleaning tack, grooming horses, stuffing hay into feeding nets, mucking stalls, preparing treats, and hauling heavy loads of soiled bedding via wheelbarrow to be dumped in the rubbish pile. But she clearly loves every minute of it.

As I watch Jenny and Mambo going through their paces, I am struck by the fluid, graceful, and balanced way Jenny rides, so I asked her about her training background. She told me that she began riding around the age of ten and was schooled in the German method, where riders are started either bareback or with a saddle but without reins or stirrups until they have achieved the correct balance and frame. Once they have, they have earned the right to have reins and stirrups, but by that point the riders are so good they don't really need either one. During her training, she rode several horses until Mambo came into her life.

Next, I asked her about her first few rides on Mambo. You can tell from his gaits that he has extremely powerful movement, and I asked her if she found him difficult to ride at first.

She responded that, as I suspected, Mambo is not easy to ride. It isn't because he's not well-behaved, but he has a giant gallop and can accelerate in a heartbeat. His trot too is springy and powerful, and it takes tremendous skill to stay with his movement. And because he is a stallion, he still takes notice of mares and likes to search for them when he and Jenny are riding, especially in spring, but then he gives up after a little excitement.

"I have been riding him for seven years now," she continued, "and we put in so many hours. I ride only him, and no one else but me rides him, so we've really developed as a team. We know each other by heart. I ride without a saddle a lot, so that really reinforces my balance. In the beginning, I had to adjust to his gaits, especially to his immense gallop. But now it just feels like flying."

When I asked her what her favorite type of riding was, she said that her love is dressage, but it's even better to practice dressage in the fields, where they are free. But she had also wanted to experiment with jumping, although when they first began riding together, neither of them knew much about it. So Mambo would canter to the jump and then stop, often skidding into the structures and knocking them over. Or he would dash to the side to avoid the jumps. But they kept practicing until they mastered it. And it became his one of his favorite things to do. Because of Mambo's size and weight, they aren't allowed to jump higher than three feet, but he clearly loves it.

He also loves the water, and in the summer months, Jenny and her sisters ride their horses into a shallow pond and play in the water. Mambo loves pawing at it to make it splash everywhere, and Jenny has a dream of one day vacationing with him by the shore and swimming in the sea.

The more I communicated with Jenny and her mom and watched Jenny's, her sisters', and their family's videos posted to YouTube, the more I came to admire and respect their family bond. Angelika and her husband have created a beautiful life for their three children, filled with unconditional love and support but balanced by dedication to work and family. And what's obvious in the life they have chronicled is that they are the five Musketeers. All for one and one for all.

After our interview, I tuned into Mambo to connect with him. I asked him about his journey with Jenny and especially his time in the forest.

I was confused. I never really knew who was coming to see me or when. People would come see me every day. But I felt isolated. And I was terrified that I would never see her again. Each time Jenny and her mom came back to see me, I felt as though I would collapse from relief. Like when a human's knees give way. But I don't think I ever really showed that.

"What did you think the day they drove up with the trailer? Jenny said she thinks you knew you were going home to the barn where you had been boarded."

I knew my worries were over.

"How would you describe your relationship with Jenny, beyond the obvious fact that you love her deeply?"

It's energizing. Uplifting. Challenging.

"Challenging?" That wasn't an answer I expected to hear.

She's the reason I work.

His answer still confused me. Because he clearly loves everything about their riding. So I probed again. "You look at this as work?"

No. It's a good thing. She keeps me at my peak. There's a push and pull to be better, and that friction ignites my soul.

I love it. I love the challenge. I am my best version of myself because of her.

"What do you love most about her?"

She brings out the best in me, but she lets me be who I am. She pushes me to be better, but it's always with respect in regard to who I am and what I can do. It's like she creates the space for me to improve but lets me step into it on my own. I get to be amazing because of her. My true potential is realized with her. I have a new life, like being hatched anew from an egg. We have new beginnings every day. She is my universe.

I asked Jenny what Mambo had taught her, and she replied that he has taught her how strong a friendship with an animal can be. But she went on to say that he is more than a friend for her. He is her life. She understands what it means to take responsibility for an animal. Nothing is as important to her as Mambo is. She doesn't need fame, even though she has it. She doesn't need to be successful, even though she is. She only wants to be with Mambo, and she wants both of them to be happy and healthy. So she works tirelessly to make that so. And Mambo gives back to her in return.

She has one video titled "We Were Young, We Were Wild, We Were Halfway Free." It's a charming montage of Jenny and Mambo galloping bareback through the forests and fields using only a rope around his neck to communicate with him, cantering in the show ring in her classic black and white dressage attire, and reliving the moment when her parents gifted Mambo to her. And yes, there are a couple of kisses thrown in for good measure.

What most people see when they watch her videos is a fairytale. A love story. And I see that too. But beyond that what I see is an enchanting horse who loves and respects his person and a young woman who honors, respects, and loves her horse for who he is. And because of that, he is young, wild, and *completely* free.

Note: One of the humorous things about writing this story is that I don't speak German, and Jenny and her mom speak only a little English. But we muddled through our communications using Google Translate, which would some-times make incorrect and comical substitutions. One day, I remembered that my riding instructor was from Austria and could speak German. So she became our interpreter when Google Translate failed us. Thank you, Dagmar, for your help in bringing this beautiful story to fruition.

֍ ♡ ֍

For more information on Jenny and Mambo, visit their social media channels:

Facebook:
https://www.facebook.com/Mambo-283915748338649/

YouTube:
https://www.youtube.com/user/fabilein93?feature=guide

Jenny and Mambo are featured on the back cover of this book. The photo was shot by Mona Doerre of Mona Doerre Photography. For more information on Mona Doerre and her photography, visit www.monadoerre.de.

Tragically, Mambo suffered an accident just weeks before *Devotion* was published. His injuries made it impossible for him to walk or stand. And the family made the painful but necessary decision to euthanize him. Mambo passed away in Jenny's arms, and her heartbreaking but beautiful tribute to her boy was posted to Facebook the following day:

Our time has been much too short, despite the seven years we've had together. For over three years, I was able to proudly call this horse "my own." Now he has been torn from my life but not my heart. Mambo, I will always love you and hold pride and honor in my heart that you were mine. I am infinitely grateful for everything! You were the best and most unique horse I could ever dream of! I wish I could turn back time and spend many wonderful years with you! But it was not to be. Now you can gallop with your friends in Heaven as you had always done down here on Earth. Someday we will see each other again, and then we will do everything for which we had no more chances to do now.

Nemo and Denise

It was a grey, dismal, wind-whipped day in late December. The weather mirrored the news we were to hear next. We had been contacted by a local shelter. An older German Shepherd Dog had come in weeks ago as a stray and in very poor health. Because of his condition, he would be released only to a rescue, and two others had already declined. Nemo had forty-eight hours to live, and he needed a Christmas miracle.

One of our volunteers, Denise, went to the shelter to meet the dog and do an evaluation. She walked through the doors and was ushered down the cold, concrete corridor and then to a small holding yard at the rear of the shelter. What she saw next horrified her. A massive, almost hairless male German Shepherd lumbered slowly, painfully toward her. His body was covered with oozing scars and open sores. It was one of the worst cases of mange she'd ever seen.

Half of his fur was gone, exposing immense patches of grey, ravaged skin, and he had a musty odor from a secondary yeast infection, a result of his condition being left untreated for so long. His wrinkled, hairless muzzle hung slack, and his paws were severely compromised. The mange had manifested blisters and deep wounds between his paw pads and they bled. His right front leg was swollen, and he couldn't bend the elbow. Walking caused him extreme pain. Denise's knees buckled, and she placed her hand on the wall to steady herself. Tears filled her eyes, and she choked back sobs. She'd never seen a dog in such horrific shape.

She sat next to him and gazed into his eyes. Nemo met her gaze with empty hopelessness, almost as if he knew his time was limited and his fate had already been determined. As though he'd given up and no longer cared. She found an area on his side that had been spared. Where fur still clung to his otherwise bald and scarred body. She started to pet him. And massage his ears.

"Moments later, he looked into my eyes and leaned into me. A glimmer of hope replaced the blank stare." She whispered a promise. That he would be loved from this day forth. That she would care for him and find him a perfect home. That she would be his champion. And so their love affair began.

"I named Nemo for the little fish in the Disney movie who became lost in a big, scary ocean," she said. "Because I felt this dog was alone in a big and scary world."

Nemo had become lost, a dog in need, wallowing in a sea of hundreds of other dogs stranded in the harsh reality of the shelter system, where he'd languished, was repeatedly overlooked, and risked euthanization due to his condition. Luckily, that didn't come to pass. But Nemo's journey was just beginning. He had months of recovery ahead.

Denise completed the paperwork, pulled him from the shelter, and then drove directly to her vet. Nemo was diagnosed with Demodectic mange, a condition in which mites live in the hair follicles and oil glands of the skin. It could have been treated, but because it was not, Nemo had developed a secondary infection that had to be treated with antibiotics. He was poked and prodded repeatedly. There were blood tests and vaccinations, and he was immobilized for X-rays.

The biggest surprise was that his during his vet check, a dental exam revealed that he was just eighteen months old, not five years old as the shelter had estimated. Through it all, Nemo was brave, curious, gentle, grateful, and fearless. He seemed to know that every step and every procedure was to his benefit. He seemed to know that these strange new people were trying to help him. Later he was sedated so the vet could shave him and treat the mange. Finally, after hours at the vet, he was ready to go to his new home with Denise.

"I decided to foster him myself," she said. "I didn't want him to go through any more change. I decided it would be my good deed for the holiday season. I thought I would be giving him a gift. Little did I know that it would be I who would be receiving the gift."

Once home and settled in with Denise, Nemo began his intensive healing process. He required daily medicated baths. He had to be scrubbed, and the process caused his already-tender skin to bleed. In an attempt to make his baths semi-tolerable, Denise massaged his scabs. As the motion and water softened them, chunks of dead skin fell away and rinsed down the drain.

Compounding the unsavory process was the fact that it was winter, and even in sunny San Diego, winters can be cold. The shampoo had to remain on Nemo for fifteen minutes after being applied, and even though the bath water was warm, Nemo endured discomfort as his wet body cooled in the bathroom. Denise dragged heaters into the bathroom to attempt to warm it. But we all know the chill of stepping out of the shower soaking wet. The whole experience was unpleasant and uncomfortable.

Once the shampoo had set long enough, Nemo was rinsed, and a hydrating skin serum was applied. It too had to sit for fifteen minutes. Then he was rinsed once more, and iodine was applied to his blistered feet and neck. This process went on for months. The perfect patient through it all, Nemo was quiet and tolerant and never complained. He gratefully endured the poking, prodding, and scrubbing as he sat patiently in the tub, part drowned rat, part regal-Shepherd-to-be.

When Denise first brought Nemo into her home, she and her husband were careful about socializing Nemo with their other two dogs. But they quickly saw that he was dog-friendly and extremely respectful of her dogs. So within days, he was at liberty in their house. Even their male Shepherd, Kayu, a rescue as well, who hated all male dogs, was almost instantly friendly with Nemo. The pack of three had assimilated beautifully.

"I think my dogs felt sorry for him," Denise said. "It was so apparent that he needed us. My husband and I had planned to travel and be with family over the holidays, but we canceled our plans. We knew Nemo needed us. And we knew we had to be there for him."

After five weeks, Nemo began to show progress. His daily baths had dropped to tri-weekly. The open sores were mending, and the swelling on his paws and neck were greatly reduced. Gone was the incessant itching and scratching. Gone was the unpleasant smell of the infection. A month later, he needed baths only once a week, but because of the severity of his condition, he'd need treatment for an additional eight to ten weeks.

"What made this so scary was how advanced his condition was in the beginning," Denise said. "I knew that in rare cases Demodex could be life-threatening, and Nemo was just so compromised. I'd never had a dog in such a miserable state and requiring so much physical care. I worried about him not making it. Had he not survived…that would have broken my heart. All other dogs I fostered or adopted or bought from a breeder were healthy. This was a true test of my skills and mental fortitude."

Nemo's will to live was strong, even though he was sick and vulnerable. And the hope that Denise had first seen in his eyes grew with each day they spent together. Denise and her husband learned quickly that Nemo hated to be alone, and despite his mangled paws, he followed them everywhere, taking slow, labored steps so he could be near them. Because his skin was still fragile and painful, he couldn't romp and play. Instead, he sat dutifully watching Denise's dogs scamper and roughhouse in the yard. If being a bystander reminded Nemo of his limitations, he never showed it, nor did he have any aggression toward Denise's other two dogs.

At one point in his life, Nemo must have been loved and well-cared-for. He was housebroken, he never "counter-surfed" for food scraps, he didn't jump or bark, and he never caused any problems in Denise's care. He knew basic commands and constantly looked to Denise for leadership.

As he healed in her home, Denise could see that Nemo loved to be close to his humans and was a very affectionate boy. At first, he had been too sick and sore to play with her dogs. Toys and balls held no interest for him. But eventually, Nemo's hair started to grow back and his health began to return, as well as his energy and vitality. As the weeks passed, he seemed to enjoy being part of a pack. His only issue was being slightly protective of his food. But given his past, you couldn't blame him.

Other than that, he was an ideal dog. Laid back, quiet, and well-mannered when his family lounged in the backyard or watched television. But he was becoming more energetic, and when it was time for play now, he was game. He loved walks and was a pro at chasing balls. And unlike many Shepherds, Nemo would actually retrieve the balls and bring them back.

Each day, he became more comfortable in his newly healing skin, and hints of his personality continued to emerge. Nemo discovered that he loved toys! Plush toys, squeaky toys, rubber toys. He'd play with anything and loved entertaining himself.

Crate time too caused no problems. He would often crawl into his crate and nap several times a day. Once he settled into his new routine, he didn't even mind being crated for a few hours. Now almost fully healed, he was eating "like a horse" and following his new humans around like a shadow. He also slept through the night quietly, waiting until Denise and her husband were awake to get out of his crate.

And he was creative. "Being the big boy that he was," Denise said, "my diminutive doggie door was not working for him. He couldn't get through it without getting stuck. So he pushed the entire screen door out. Problem solved! He's highly intelligent. And overall just a confident, respectful, affectionate boy."

When Denise made her daily visit to the rescue's kennels to exercise dogs waiting to be adopted, Nemo traveled with her, happy to hang out and relax in a long dog run while he watched the comings, goings, and playtime of the other rescue dogs. And when Nemo became friendly with a female dog in the run next to his, he often enjoyed romps in the play yard with her. The rescue rumor mill lit up with the news that Nemo had found a girlfriend!

Once he fully recovered, Nemo became a strong and powerful boy determined to fulfill his Shepherd legacy and protect his humans and his property. But because of his imposing size and burgeoning energy, Denise felt that in his new home he would need a structured and disciplined environment with a well-settled dog to continue to model good manners.

"If we could find that for him," she said, "I knew that he would be an amazing addition to the right family. So I made sure that his bio on the rescue website reflected that. I even joked about the lucky family that would 'find Nemo.'"

By the end of May, Nemo's energy continued to increase. He began to investigate Denise's backyard pool, poking at the water with his nose and eventually diving headlong into the deep end. Swimming became one of his favorite activities, perhaps washing away the memories of every uncomfortable medicated bath he'd endured. He continued to come into his own and develop more confidence. Even though his coat was still patchy and he'd yet to fully achieve his potential beauty, Nemo was never self-conscious about his looks. Denise described him as a King Shepherd, extremely robust and muscular in stature with a self-confident, well-balanced personality bereft of shyness or nervousness. A dog who was eager to please and friendly to every dog encountered, large and small. A dog who was gentle with children and cats.

"It was clear we had a very special dog on our hands," Denise said.

In June, Nemo was ready to take his place in the rescue. Ready to look for a forever home. And ready to be found. There were times when Denise considered adopting him herself. But one day, Nemo was invited for a visit by the parents of one of our volunteers.

They were looking for a very special dog: a German Shepherd Dog with excellent temperament; a dog who would be dog-, cat-, and bird-friendly; a dog who would be gentle with children and responsive to all family members and friends. The lucky dog they chose would have more than an acre of land covered in lush green grass on which to run and play with four new canine companions, a swimming pool in which to cool off, and, of course, love and attention from many dog lovers. Nemo had a few tests to pass, and pass them he did. In Denise's words, Nemo had won the adoption lottery.

Perhaps one of Denise's greatest joys is that she didn't have to say goodbye to Nemo once he was adopted. She lives next door to the son of the family who adopted him, so every time Nemo visits the son, Denise and her dogs have an iron-clad play date.

I tuned into Nemo months after he'd found his forever home and asked him what being with Denise had meant to him.

I was honored to have met her. She plucked me from a gaping pit of despair and made me right again. Whole again. Free again. She healed me and gave me wings.

When I asked him what he hoped we humans could learn from our animal companions, he said that he wished humans could understand that animal companions are not things or possessions or something to tire of and then abandon.

Humans are not more important than animals even though many act that way. The commitment to an animal companion should be no different than the promises and commitment that the best and most devoted parents make to their children when they bring them into the world. The role of caretaker is sacred.

Today, you'd never recognize Nemo. Gone is the scaly, blistered, oozing skin. Gone is the patchy, scruffy coat. Gone are the swollen, blistered feet. Nemo is now a massive, stunning, silky-coated, black-and-tan Shepherd. Huge in stature and presence. What remains constant is his beautiful, loving heart; his sharp mind; his calm, regal demeanor; and his devoted soul.

I asked Denise what Nemo meant to her. She replied, "Nemo reminded me that animals and humans share similar traits, such as patience and tolerance. Animals can trust humans in a way that humans sometimes find it hard to do with each other. They really are miraculous in that way."

Nemo had been a gift to her family. He came to them when he needed a Christmas miracle. And so they put their holiday plans on hold, without question, simply because Nemo needed them, and they wanted to be there for him. It was a wonderful Christmas season for all. And truly a labor of love.

Denise told me that she believed that Nemo came into her life because they needed each other. He needed a family to care for him and help him heal. And Denise needed the chance to be a caretaker again. In her home country of Brazil, Denise had been a physician. Her life revolved around caring for others and healing them. Taking care of animals and people had always been a constant in her life. But she wasn't able to practice medicine in the United States. And it had left a void in her life. She missed being a healer and making people whole and well again. Being of service empowers her. And in caring for Nemo, she was fulfilled—body, mind, and soul.

Roscoe and Mauricio

"I knew I was slowing down. But I didn't know the extent to which this disease would alter my life. And I had no idea that this dog, this miracle dog, would come out of nowhere and give me a fighting chance."

When he was just eighteen, Mauricio was diagnosed with a chronic congenital illness for which there is no cure. Called Charcot-Marie-Tooth (CMT) disease, it is one of the most commonly inherited neurological disorders. Affecting approximately 1 in 2,500 people in the United States, it preys on both motor and sensory nerves. Over time, simple activities such as speaking, walking, breathing, and swallowing become more and more difficult. In the later stages of the disease, weakness and muscle atrophy can spread to the legs and feet, which make walking difficult, and to the hands, making grasping objects, taking pills, and even closing doors a challenge.

The disease forced Mauricio's early retirement at the age of thirty-two from his job as a sportswear salesman. Before that, and despite his dismal prognosis, he was an active man—running, cycling, and often competing in races.

But over time, the disease forced him to slow down. And he regressed from running, to cycling, to walking, to riding a tricycle to stay active.

"I retired from my career because I couldn't drive, not because I couldn't function. Granted, I was becoming less and less functional, but I could still do things. I was just weaker. Tired. Less coordinated."

Enter Roscoe. A dog Mauricio met by accident. Roscoe was kept at a home next door to one of Mauricio's friends, who told him he must come and meet the dog.

"I'm not sure why he insisted," Mauricio said. "I wasn't looking for a dog, and this dog was basically a dialed-down version of Cujo."

Roscoe, originally named Lucifer Mohamed by his owners, was a thirteen-month-old, curly-haired black Lab. While smallish in stature, his demeanor was a testament to his name, and he lunged at his enclosure, grasping the chain link in his teeth and tearing at it to free himself. The only time he wasn't in his enclosure was when his people took him out to chain him to a tree during the day. At night, halogen lights beat down on him relentlessly. Because he was wild and unsocialized, his people feared him; his only interaction with them was when they maneuvered him away from his tether at the tree and wrestled him back into his cage with his food. No wonder he was almost mad.

"Imagine that your world view is a deck attached to a house," Mauricio said. "Your people rarely come out, and when they do, either they stand on the deck and ignore you or they're terrified of you. No one ever pets you. You're confined one way or another 24/7, and when you're trying to sleep, you've got a spotlight in your face. It's like being in a concentration camp. When they'd put him back in his cage at night to eat his food, he'd gulp it to try to turn and beat them to the gate before they slammed it in his face. It's unfathomable. When I first saw him, I was heartbroken. Intimidated, and a bit fearful, but heartbroken."

Mauricio told me that when he met Roscoe for the first time, something clicked. He saw something in those sad eyes. A light that flickered deep within, indicating that this dog hadn't given up. A light that Mauricio recognized in himself, stemming from his own life challenges. That day, he played with Roscoe while he was tethered. And a bond was formed.

On his second visit, with the owner's permission, he took Roscoe for a walk on the expansive property that skirted a lake. On his third visit, the owners allowed him to let Roscoe off leash to run at liberty. He threw sticks in the lake for him to retrieve and gave the beautiful dog the first taste of true freedom he'd had in many months.

"We ran. We played," Mauricio said, recalling his first visits with the exuberant pup. "And when I called him, he came right to me, almost knocking me down and covering me with kisses," he said. "And any thoughts or concerns about my disease disappeared. We were free, and I was a kid again. I realized that I needed this dog and he needed me."

After the third visit, Mauricio appealed to the owners, asking them to allow "Lucifer" to come home with him for good. Mercifully, they agreed.

"His first few moments in our home were amazing to watch. He ran around everywhere so joyfully, poking his nose in every nook and cranny, sniffing the sofa and pillows, wagging his tail like crazy, smacking it into things. It was as though everything he saw was so delightful. He's like that to this day. Everything just makes him happy."

Once home with Mauricio, it took nine months for Roscoe to settle into his new routine. He knew nothing about living in a house. He chewed his way through crates, had accidents, tore up toys, and had massive separation anxiety. But Mauricio and his partner, John, worked with Roscoe tirelessly.

"His life became consumed with training. We trained constantly to establish the structure and routine that we knew would ultimately ease his stress-related issues. And he went everywhere with me. I attached his leash to my belt, and he'd follow me around."

Mauricio and John live in a historic neighborhood in Florida. Streets lined with statuesque trees shading quaint bungalows give the neighborhood grace and charm. But fenced yard space comes at a premium, and the only place they had to train Roscoe safely off leash was an enclosed dirt median flanking their neighbor's property. The neighbor, a crotchety elderly woman with little patience, took offense to their training, claiming it was destroying the lawn. And she took them to court in an effort to keep them out of the area.

"Well, there was no lawn. It had always been a strip of dirt. We had pictures. Since we hadn't destroyed anything and we could prove it, we won the court battle she started. But the whole thing took almost a year to resolve. Once we did, we resumed training. By then, I was really slowing down. Still able-bodied, but slowing down."

Although still able to care for himself, Mauricio knew it was only a matter of time before the disease caused him to atrophy further, and he began to ponder the prospect of training Roscoe to be a service dog. So in 2005 he began looking for trainers. Which proved to be a challenge. In their area, neither service dogs nor trainers were common. But after months of searching, Mauricio found a trainer at a conference.

"Most people would have thought I was nuts," he said. "I mean, the criteria for a service dog at the bare minimum is 'Is your dog comfortable in every thinkable situation? Can your dog cope with all kinds of people and dogs and all kinds of animals? Is your dog non-aggressive and non-protective?' When we first met Roscoe, he was none of those things, but he'd been with us for three years, and his anxiety and aggression were a thing of the past. And we already had the basics down cold. Now it was a matter of teaching him to open and close doors, keep an eye on me, bark if I fell or couldn't move, retrieve pill bottles. Simple things like that."

Well into their first year, training still posed a challenge. Walking with Roscoe was more like being pulled. On days when Mauricio was tired, he'd ride a scooter tricycle. But Roscoe was a young, exuberant, and still-excitable boy, and there were many times when he would pull too fast or get worked up about chasing the neighborhood cat and topple the trike. After three years, Roscoe was ready to be tested. The timing coincided with the fact that Mauricio's health had deteriorated to the point that Roscoe's skills were very much needed.

"When we took him for testing," Mauricio recalls, "he didn't pass. They felt he wasn't ready. Close but not quite. But they gave him a passing grade anyway because a second fail would have given us no options. And the evaluators felt so confident that as a team we would progress."

Despite his challenges, Mauricio tries to make a difference. For his family, his friends, and his community. He spends time volunteering in local political campaigns. And in his own neighborhood, he had started to raise funds and support to build a dog park that was handicap-accessible for scooters and wheelchairs. Complete with electric doors that open themselves, and water fountains and benches at the correct height. The initiative didn't succeed, but Mauricio finds a silver lining in the failed plan.

"Parks and Rec is more aware now of the need, so someday it might happen. I felt like it heightened the need to provide more services and access in general for the handicapped, and that's definitely a good thing."

When I asked him about his daily routine, his response was, "Then or now?" It was a sobering question that made me pause. Made me ponder the reality of what his life had been like before and what it was now. Made me consider in that split second what I took for granted and what I should be grateful for.

He said that the early days were about bonding, training, and being together. Taking daily walks, working on a communication system. Now their pace is lower-key, and as Mauricio's condition worsens, his mobility becomes more challenged.

"I can't be alone. There's a lot I can't do for myself. On a typical day, it's really just about the basics—sleeping, bathing, eating. But Roscoe helps me keep it all in perspective. And he keeps me honest. I'm not supposed to climb up to get things because I wear braces on my legs, but that dog, he catches me every time I do something I shouldn't and barks until I get down or get busted by John." Then he chuckled.

"This dog is my everything. He's my arms, my legs, my mobility. My alarm clock even." He chuckled again. "If he wakes before I do, he licks me awake and jumps on the bed with a toy in his mouth. Then it's breakfast time. Then, if I'm feeling up to it, I might get on my scooter and take him for a walk. After that, I shower. He closes the door for me and barks to get someone to help if I can't get out. He'll retrieve my pills if I need them. He's my lifeline for sure."

Roscoe also forces Mauricio to chill. Both require morning and afternoon naps, although Mauricio used to resist them. He knows now that if he doesn't rest, neither will Roscoe, and the dog will become overly tired and wound up. So at 11:00 and 2:00, the team crashes for a nap.

"If I even move, he'll immediately rouse himself, and his sleep will be ruined. So I force myself to lie still and rest so that he can. When I'm sick, he'll lie with me all day. It's the most comforting thing ever."

Beyond his illness, Mauricio has endured many struggles. He's a first-generation American in a family from Costa Rica. And he's no stranger to discrimination. He's battled the HIV virus successfully for more than twenty-two years. His race, sexual orientation, and disability are challenges that he faces willingly. All because his dog makes him believe he can do anything.

Recently, a cab driver refused to pick him up because he was traveling with Roscoe, which is a violation of the Americans with Disabilities Act (ADA). The cabbie demanded to see proof of Roscoe's service dog certification. Mauricio calmed himself, asserted his rights, and claimed his cab ride. On another occasion, he was waiting for a city bus when his legs seized up. He called out for help, but no one came. He called an ambulance on his own and traveled to the hospital with Roscoe looking over him.

"I try to take it all in stride," he said. "That's what Roscoe's taught me. I remember one time, it was a few years after 9/11, that Roscoe and I were taking a late-night walk when the police stopped us for questioning. I was understandably nervous, even though I hadn't done anything, because it just seemed like everyone was so hyper-vigilant that it was causing stress and overreaction. So I didn't know what to expect. Roscoe could tell how nervous I was. That dog sensed my fear and glued himself to me. He'll do it other times when we're out and he can tell that I'm insecure about something. He'll lick me or nudge me or bark, and it breaks my pattern. It grounds me and redirects my fear."

When I tuned in to Roscoe to ask him what his connection to Mauricio meant to him, he said that when their eyes met for the first time, he felt that he'd found his soulmate. That Mauricio understood him.

He wasn't fearful. He was the first one. And somehow, I knew he needed me. And then, when I began helping him live his life...be mobile...retain his independence, it gave me a purpose I never imagined. Serving him and helping him makes me fulfilled.

"When I think about your first home compared to the life you have with Mauricio...I mean, it's night and day."

What do you mean by night and day?

"Sorry. Human slang. I mean the two life experiences are the opposite of one another. How would you compare it?"

There is no comparison. Humans who can't integrate their animals into their everyday lives shouldn't have any. My first family's treatment of me was abusive. Just because I wasn't beaten didn't mean I wasn't abused. I had no connection to them, physical or otherwise. And it was painful. Humans need to understand how much we crave their emotional and physical connection. It's how we heal each other. And make each other whole.

Later, when I asked Mauricio what he thought he'd learned from Roscoe, he paused and said that it was a wakeup call to not judge people, although he added that people often judge him. "You can't judge someone's character by their outward appearance. When I first met Roscoe, he was wild. If I'd let that initial impression sway me, we would have never gone forward and I would never have had this boy in my life."

Then he paused and said that ultimately Roscoe was a reminder to find the joy in life.

"He's so joyful. Always. And I don't care how sad I am, it changes my outlook. But it's more than that. When I'm with him, I'm not crippled. If I'm out without him, and I feel shaky or insecure, I'm completely vulnerable. He makes me strong. He's changed my outlook on life. He's taught me patience. He's taught me to laugh more. But ultimately, he makes me realize that even in my state, I'm whole."

As I reflected upon his words, I saw such truth in them. Dogs don't care whether we're rich or poor. Whether we can run a marathon or need a scooter. Whether we live in a palace or a tent. They just want to be with us, and they love us for exactly what and who we are. There's a saying that dogs are not our whole lives but they make our lives whole. For Mauricio, that saying would read: dogs *are* our whole lives because they make us whole.

Note: A year after I had finished writing his story, Mauricio reached out to me via email. Roscoe had begun to slow down, and Mauricio had been gifted a new therapy dog, a beautiful, plush, copper-coated retriever. He and Roscoe and bonded deeply, and Roscoe retired into the less-demanding role of companion dog. Just months before the publication of this book, Mauricio contacted me again, telling me that an unexpected illness had claimed Roscoe's life. He was devastated but grateful to have had the love, support, and memories of his gifted and beloved Roscoe.

Felicity and Patti

"I wasn't looking for a horse when I found her," Patti said. "I just wanted to give back, so I had been volunteering at a horse rescue. And we thought the exposure to horses might be helpful for our adopted, special-needs daughter, Sarah. One day I saw Felicity. And we stared into each other's eyes. I was rooted in place." Then she paused and her voice cracked slightly. "Maybe it was she who found me."

Patti and I boarded our horses together on the same ranch. She'd moved her horses there a few years after I had, but we'd never really become close. I tended to lose myself in the company of my horse, Bear.

One day, I walked past Patti as she groomed Felicity in the barn aisle, and I stopped to say hello and give Felicity, her milk-chocolate-colored Quarter Horse a pat. Patti asked me how I was.

"Tired," I replied and explained that I'd just launched my second book and was fried. When she asked me what my book was about, I told her I was an amateur animal communicator and the stories were about lessons I'd learned from the animals I had met.

"You too?" she asked. "I've been communicating for years. I've always talked to them. I don't tell very many people, though."

"Yeah, I'm so used to talking about it now, though, I forget to censor. Generally, people are interested when I tell them. But I still get a few cocked heads and raised eyebrows."

"Right. No one wants to be known as the crazy lady who thinks she can talk to animals."

I smiled at her and nodded. And she began to tell me her story.

Patti had taken her daughter to FalconRidge Equine Rescue, a horse sanctuary nestled in the inland San Diego County foothills just a few miles from the ranch where we boarded our horses. They'd been introduced to the sanctuary by a friend who felt working with horses might be a therapeutic outlet for Sarah. They'd traveled to the sanctuary a few times to visit. Then Sarah began taking lessons on a thirty-four-year-old Quarter Horse whose name, ironically, was also Sarah.

"She was a healing horse," Patti said. "And I know Sarah bonded with her even more deeply since they shared the same name. With each lesson, I saw my daughter begin to come out of her shell. Her body would loosen up and relax as she allowed herself to move with the horse's rhythm. I saw my daughter express emotion for the first time when riding the horse."

One day at the rescue, a volunteer with Felicity in tow walked past Patti. The horse stopped mid-stride and fixed Patti her gentle gaze. Patti turned to her husband and said, "I have to have her. I think she will be just what Sarah needs."

Felicity had come to FalconRidge Equine Rescue when her owner passed away. Before that, she'd been a family horse, happily chauffeuring her elderly companion on trail rides through the sagebrush. Upon his death, he willed Felicity to his children, who relinquished her to FalconRidge in hopes that they could find an appropriate home for her. Her quiet, gentle demeanor made her a perfect therapy horse. And she seemed to revel in working with children.

"She's drawn to children," Patti said. "I think she picks up on their innocence. Sarah and I both bonded with her quickly. She's helped both of us to heal. I was severely injured as a kid when I was thrown from a horse. So, as much as I loved horses and ached to ride again, I was afraid. At the sanctuary, one of the volunteers urged me to ride Felicity, and this girl won my confidence to the point where I thought I could give it a try."

On her first ride, Patti swung her leg over Felicity's back, settled in the saddle, held the reins in one hand, and then gripped the pommel of the saddle with the other, not moving for the longest time. When Felicity felt Patti was ready, she gingerly took one step forward and then another. With every step, Patti felt herself relax.

"I realized tears were streaming down my face. And then sobs as I released the pain and fear of the past and embraced the sheer joy of reconnecting with a horse again. When I got off of her, I saw that her eyes were watering too. I knew my healing had begun. And in that moment what I realized was how intuitive this horse was. How deeply she felt what I felt."

"I think all creatures are that way," I said. "They're just waiting for the human race to wake up and interact with them on a deeper level." I paused and then asked, "What was Sarah's life like before she came to you?"

Patti took a deep breath and started to tell me Sarah's story. Sarah was a victim of abuse and neglect from the day she was born. She and her birth mother had emigrated from the Kosovo refugee camps. They lived with a few others in a mobile home. But within a week of arriving in the states, Sarah's mom and the others vanished. Abandoned, Sarah was left on her own. A helpless infant with no choice other than to lie flat on her back in her crib. So much time passed that the back of her head flattened, restricting the flow of fluid to her brain and stunting its cellular development. When help did come, Sarah's rescuers found her emaciated, a bag of bones lying in her own waste.

"Those first few weeks in an infant's life are such a critical development period. Bonding and attachment happen between mother and child through touch and other non-verbal connection. But Sarah got none of that. Or not enough," Patti said.

Sarah had been emotionally starved. And as a result, she learned not to love or trust or attach emotionally with anyone. She learned to wall herself off. In her world, love equaled pain, and it was better to keep those who might hurt you at a distance than to risk opening up to hurt and disappointment again.

When Sarah was about eighteen months old, her biological mother reappeared, demanding to be reunited with her child. The foster system had no choice but to comply. Their time together lasted about a year before Sarah was back in foster care. Sarah found her way to Patti and her husband at age three and a half. Patti and her husband began fostering Sarah when they learned they couldn't have children of their own. And they hoped to eventually adopt her.

Even after everything that had happened between Sarah and her biological mother, Patti was required to squire Sarah to weekly supervised visits, in which Sarah generally escalated into violent screaming and emotional tantrums. After the visits, Sarah would often have nightmares for days. This continued for a year and a half until the biological mother backed out of Sarah's life again.

"We've made progress with her over the years," Patti said, "through the different therapies we've tried and just pouring love into her ourselves, but she has Reactive Attachment Disorder. She'll never be completely whole. It's not possible for her to attach to another human. She can develop superficial attachments, but that's it. The only thing that really brings her out of her shell, really gives her peace, is her time with the horses. Felicity has been a godsend to our entire family."

Patti and her husband were finally able to adopt Sarah when she was five and a half. Six months later, they purchased Felicity and moved her to the ranch. Ironically, it was at the same point when Sarah's brain stopped developing. Freezing her in time. As a result, she can't rationalize that her mom was an inept parent and a poor influence. Her cognitive reasoning will always be that of a six-year-old. But in the moments she spends with Felicity, she becomes so much more.

When you watch Felicity and Sarah interact, you can see what Patti is alluding to. The distraction and the go-go frenetic energy Sarah carries with her abates. Her expression softens. Her eyes fill with love, and she talks to Felicity softly, quietly, whispering as if speaking a language only they can understand.

Patti shared one of her favorite pictures of the two of them. Felicity had closed her eyes and lowered her head to Sarah's stomach, and Sarah cradled Felicity's chocolate head in her arms, a cherubic smile playing about her lips. The energy I picked up from the photo floored me. It was as though a filmy, white aura surrounded them, encircling them in a protective bubble. In that moment, frozen in time by the camera's lens, you could feel the peace flowing, river-like, through Sarah's being and hushing her fevered brain.

My connection to Felicity deepened when Patti offered to let me borrow her. It was a holiday weekend, and my brother and his family were coming to visit. My four-year-old grandniece, Sophia, is obsessed with horses, so my brother had asked me to find a stable where we could take a trail ride. Instead, I suggested finding a mellow horse at the ranch. And Felicity seemed the perfect solution.

When they arrived at my house, Sophia was practically vibrating, and she chattered excitedly, chirping like a busy bird discovering a fresh cache of seed. Ethan, her two-year-old brother who suffers from physical disabilities, was more subdued. At the ranch, I demonstrated proper grooming techniques to eyes that quickly glazed over.

Seeing their boredom, I sped the saddling process, placing just a simple riding pad on Felicity's back and fashioning a bridle from a halter and two lead lines attached at the buckles on the sides. Then I marched my protégés to the riding arena.

I hoisted Sophia to Felicity's safe, broad back and led her around the arena, teaching her to turn the mare by alternately pulling each lead line gently to the side. I looked back from time to time to make sure she was still centered on the riding pad. She was a natural, and her little body seemed to merge with Felicity's, moving in unison with every undulation of Felicity's back. A happy smile lit up her face, and you could feel joy radiating from her little body. After about thirty minutes, we stopped, and I held out my arms and helped her dismount to give Ethan his turn.

Then I lifted Ethan to Felicity's back and settled him on the riding pad, instructing his parents to walk on either side and steady him if he should start to slide. We secured his hand on the safety strap on the pad, and I began to lead Felicity at a walk. I glanced back occasionally, and his mom remarked, "I've never seen his body this loose and relaxed. And he's actually using his right hand more than he usually does. I'd heard about the benefits of therapy riding, but to see it in action is pretty powerful."

Then Ethan let out a whoop and giggled. In the two years I'd known him, I'd never heard him laugh.

I turned to the kids' mom and asked, "What was it like for you to see Sophia on her first horse? Knowing how much she loves them."

"It was surreal," she responded. "You didn't know this, but *Brave* is her favorite movie. She's watched it over and over and is especially enthralled with how the main character, Merida, becomes so independent when she's galloping her horse across her country." She lowered her voice and whispered, "When she was on Felicity, I know she became Merida. Her heroine. And it was one of the most magical moments I've ever seen."

I smiled, nodded, and then turned away, tears welling in my eyes. Felicity had connected to Sophia with her inner warrior. When I told Patti the story, she smiled and said, "Aww…that melts my heart. I love hearing that. She is happiest when she's around kids. She's a healer. Kids are her life. It's her calling."

I expressed my gratitude once again. Patti and Felicity had given my entire family a gift that we would not soon forget.

Later that year, I noticed that Sarah had stopped coming to the ranch. But I'd never asked Patti about it. The day we sat down to talk about her story, I did.

"For a while," she said, "Felicity was able to help Sarah manage her anger issues. If Sarah flared up at the ranch, Felicity would toss her head and step back or nudge her stomach with her nose, and I'd tell her, 'Felicity is telling you she doesn't like your anger. It's worrisome to her. You need to manage your moods so they don't affect others.' I didn't have that kind of influence over Sarah. But Felicity did. She helped Sarah to change for a while. But during the last two years she was with us, her anger became unmanageable. She became a danger to herself. But I couldn't give up on her. I quit my job so I could be with her. But ultimately, she thinks we took her away from her mom. And her anger stems from that. She doesn't understand that her birth mother isn't able to care for her."

"And you must get a lot of unsolicited advice," I said, "from people who don't understand Sarah's behavior."

"Oh, you wouldn't believe the things other parents, other people say to us. And the judgment we deal with. It's one of the reasons I started counseling other moms like me."

After battling Sarah's anger for more than eight years, the last two being almost impossible, the situation became too much for Patti and her husband. For Patti's safety, they eventually made the heart-breaking decision to place her in a facility. After months there, Sarah began to stabilize. Patti and her husband visit Sarah every Sunday and take her pictures of Felicity.

"Those two years…the final two…they must have been horrific," I said. "Emerging from it must have felt like PTSD."

"It was. And beyond that, there was guilt associated with feeling like I had PTSD. I felt only warriors deserved that badge of courage and honor."

"There are all kinds of warriors," I offered. "And all kinds of battles."

She nodded, and then continued. "I got so tired of feeling like I was reinventing myself and my identity. My identity had been so connected to my job. When I quit to care for Sarah in those last two years, my identity then became being Sarah's caregiver 24/7. And even though I didn't have my career, I had a new identity. I was Sarah's guardian. Her coach. Her brain. And it was important. With Sarah gone, I didn't know who I was. It's exhausting to try to reinvent again."

"You should probably give yourself time to heal. The new identity will emerge when you're healed. Maybe your purpose now is simply to take care of yourself," I said.

Patti is still coping with her last few years with Sarah. Coping with feeling like a failure, even though she did everything in her power to save Sarah. Coping with the exhaustion that clung to her like damp clothing. Coping with the depression that threatened to suck her into a grey, meaningless fog. And in coping, her connection to the special horse who'd battled with her to save her daughter deepened. Patti's daily visits to the ranch gave her life meaning and a reason to go on. She'd saddle Felicity, and they'd amble out on long trail rides, wandering up a stretch of road to a hill that looked out over an expansive valley, and there, they'd bask in the view.

"It was like an addiction. But a positive one. I had to go to the ranch. I had to see that horse. I couldn't skip a day. She balanced me. She helped me fight the depression. She gave me purpose. She relieved my stress. She was my lifeline. In the beginning of our relationship, she helped me conquer my fear of horses. In the end, she just saved me."

One morning, Patti got a call from the barn manager. Felicity was off. Not moving well. Patti called the vet to meet her at the ranch, but by the time Patti arrived, Felicity had collapsed. When Felicity saw Patti running toward her, she tried to stand. She took one step and collapsed, struggled to her feet, took another step, and collapsed again. Patti rushed to her side and sat with her to keep her from moving. When the vet arrived, together they got her up and moving to the vet's truck.

"I knew with each step she took, that horse was telling me she wasn't done. Telling me not to give up on her. So we tried everything. Checked everything. The ultrasound showed no damage, no broken bones. It was baffling. The only thing I could think of is that she'd run hard in the arena when I turned her out the day before. Maybe she'd tightened up overnight to the point where she couldn't move. In that moment, I promised her I'd find a solution. Hours later, she was able to walk but still with some stiffness."

Patti tried many remedies after that. Chiropractic work, stretching exercises, massage. She promised Felicity she'd keep researching until she found something that worked. Finally, after two years of experimenting with treatments, she remembered an energy worker she'd met during her time at FalconRidge. The woman worked with horses on an emotional, spiritual, and physical level. Patti sent her a text asking her to come and help.

The energy worker ran her hands over Felicity, hovering over her hip, and then pushed her side. The hip joint made a loud popping sound like a cork being released from a champagne bottle. The mare relaxed, and the woman continued to work on Felicity's body like she was clearing cobwebs, drawing wisps of energy from her and lightly massaging her body. Felicity nuzzled her and played with the zipper on her coat. When she was done, the energy worker tuned into Felicity and told Patti what she'd learned.

"This horse has huge emotional issues. She feels like she failed Sarah because she didn't heal her, so she feels that she's not good enough. She also tells me that you told her you wouldn't give up until you found someone to help her. You kept your promise."

Four visits later, Felicity's balance was restored and the pair resumed their trail rides.

"I thought I'd never ride her again. I was reconciled to that, but it's a gift to have her back. And even though we were never able to balance Sarah mentally and emotionally, Felicity helped us to the extent that she could. She was our connection, our middle ground. When Sarah and I were in Felicity's presence, I was no longer the woman who had taken her from her biological mom."

Six months later, tragedy struck again. Felicity coliced. Colic is a deadly, fast-moving condition in which the bowels constrict, twist, and become impacted. An exam revealed her intestines were clogged with fecal matter from her hindquarters to her shoulders. Patti spent the next three days at the ranch by Felicity's side, changing the IV bags that nursed essential fluids into her, talking to her beloved horse, and praying. Her husband shuttled food and changes of clothes to her. And Patti willed Felicity to pull through.

"I told her that I wasn't ready. That she couldn't go. That I couldn't live without her."

On day four, while Patti talked to her beautiful horse, Felicity began to nibble at her food. Then she pooped. And Patti felt they might be winning the battle. The vet arrived and examined her. The blockage was gone. It was nothing short of a miracle. The severity of the situation would normally have been a death sentence. He had no medical explanation other than telling Patti she had willed Felicity to live.

As we continued to talk, I asked Patti how she'd describe Felicity. She laughed.

"Well, she's a woman of many personalities," she replied. Then her voice softened. "She's unlike any horse I've ever known. She's sarcastic, funny, caring, silly, sweet, goofy, crabby, and complex. One amazing horse wrapped up in an amazing package. She shakes it up, depending on who she's with, and she surprises me every day. She's rare. And I often wonder how I got so lucky to have her with me."

When I tapped into Felicity and asked her how she'd describe her life purpose, she showed me a picture of Dorothy from *The Wizard of Oz*, whose journey to find her way back home leads her to a diverse group of friends who band together to battle dangers and ultimately find their inner strength. I sensed that what she meant is that she too had been searching for home. A place she found when she met Patti. When I asked her to describe her connection to Patti, she showed me an infinity symbol. A powerful connection both complete and endless.

When I asked Patti what she thought Felicity was here to teach her, she responded immediately. "That animals have so much to teach us. Felicity has been with me for just a few years, and in such a short time she made such a huge impact. I can't imagine my life without her. Her purpose on earth is huge. She showed me what unconditional love was. She was the one who modeled it for me. And she still does. Every single day."

~ ♡ ~

Sidney and Victoria

"Did he just kiss you?" Victoria asked, glancing away from her view of the road briefly. Her dog Sidney had just reached forward from the back seat of the car and gingerly licked my cheek.

"Mm hmm," I said.

"That does not happen," she said. Then she repeated emphatically, "That does *not* happen. He doesn't kiss anyone except me...ever."

"Well, I just tapped into him and picked up a piece of a past life that was really important to him. He knows I just told you, and he is grateful."

Sidney is a classic, regal, black and tan German Shepherd. Strong, sinewy, and stunning, he was typically aloof, preferring to interact only with his mom, Victoria. She and I were headed to a dog party hosted by one of the volunteers in the German Shepherd rescue Victoria and I were part of, and today was the first time I had met Sidney. Since she knew I could communicate with animals, she'd asked me to read him on the drive to the party. Sidney was riding in the back, butt on the seat, paws on the floor, head in between Victoria and me. He had told me moments before that he hates being in crates because he had a past life in which he had been neglected. *Neglected.* That's a kind word for it. From the vision I'd been shown when he told me his story, he'd basically been locked in a windowless room for hours at a time when his family had been busy. And the memory was stamped into his cellular structure. As a result, any type of confinement in this life caused him great anxiety.

When it comes to dogs, Sidney is my type. He's handsome and magnetic but has an incredible sense of humor. To watch him gallop and trot in his backyard is a thing of beauty. He's powerful, fluid, and majestic. He floats when he moves.

He draws people in because of his looks, but he prefers Victoria's company over other humans. Unless they happen to have a ball to throw for him. He's obsessed with balls. Anyone who thinks dogs can't tell time has never been to Victoria's house at three o'clock. That's when "ball time" starts. It's a daily two-hour ritual during which Victoria repeatedly tosses balls in the backyard for Sidney to chase. Since Victoria works from home, Sidney is by her side all day. He starts vocalizing around 2:45 each day in case Victoria should ever forget that it will soon be time to start playing.

Sidney came into Victoria's life at a critical juncture. She'd just lost her beloved Golden Retriever, Newt. He was the love of her life, and his death devastated her.

"I just sat around crying uncontrollably. Newt had been so gorgeous and sweet and perfect. And we were such a team. It was just the two of us facing life together. I would always look into his eyes and say to him, 'I don't ever want to get married again, but if I did, I'd marry you.' He was my world."

Several days into her grieving process, a friend contacted her. His neighbor was relinquishing their two-year-old male German Shepherd. The friend wanted Victoria to consider adopting the dog. And knowing of Newt's death, he asked her if it was too soon.

"I was so raw and broken and hurt that it seemed unfathomable that I could consider adopting a dog so soon. I didn't think I *wanted* another dog yet. I wanted Newt back, and I wanted to wallow. But after a few hours of consideration, I decided I would take this dog on three conditions."

The first condition was that she needed a sign that this was meant to be. The second condition was that the dog needed to be in good physical health. The third condition was that Newt's former trainer, Shannon, needed to evaluate the dog and give her approval that they would be a good match.

After making her decision, Victoria took the ashes of Newt and her previous German Shepherd, Cay, into the backyard. Kneeling in the grass, she said through her tears, "If you've sent me this dog, you need to let me know. Give me a sign."

Her sign came the next day. Victoria is an editor, and she was on the phone with an author she rarely spoke to. Never mentioning her recent loss of Newt, she found herself asking this man whether he was a "dog person." The man's response was that the only dog he had ever had was a German Shepherd named Victoria.

Chills ran up my spine as Victoria relayed this part of her story. "What was your reaction?" I asked.

"I froze," she replied. "But I knew this was my sign, and the first condition had been met."

The next day, she arranged to meet Sidney. Ironically, when she first met him, she thought he was ugly.

"How could you have thought he was ugly?" I asked. "He's one of the most stunning dogs I've ever seen."

"He wasn't Newt," she replied.

Victoria agreed to do a vet check to make sure that Sidney's health was good. Sidney passed the test. He was in great shape. Victoria's second condition had been met.

When Sidney first arrived at Victoria's home and she let him off leash, Sidney turned into a Tasmanian devil.

"What did he do?" I asked.

"He turned my home into a combination racetrack and obstacle course. He raced around like a madman, jumping from the floor to the coffee table, then onto the sofa, then onto the loveseat, then over the back of the loveseat and back to the sofa. He jumped on the windows and grabbed papers from my desk, and books and magazines and bills, running around with them in his mouth. He was obsessed with paper. Finally, I was able to grab him and put him in the backyard so I could de-clutter the house and hide all the paper products."

Once outside, Sidney continued his rampage of destruction, overturning patio furniture, tipping over and breaking flowerpots, grabbing plants from their pots and racing around the yard with them dangling from his mouth. This continued for two hours until he wore himself out.

"I was so out of my league with this dog," she said. "With the exception of Newt, I'd gotten all of my previous dogs as puppies. So at that point I scheduled an appointment with Shannon, hoping that she would give me some reason not to take him because I wasn't sure I could handle him and I was still kind of looking for an out." The next day, the pair went to see Shannon to get her perspective. But Shannon's immediate evaluation shocked her. Shannon told Victoria that she and Sidney were going to be wonderful together.

"I was astonished to hear those words come out of her mouth. I asked her how she could know that in the brief time she had spent with us. Shannon's response was, 'Look at how he's watching you. He hasn't taken his eyes off you since you arrived. He's waiting for you to tell him what to do. He already sees you as his leader.' "

With the third condition met, Victoria needed to make good on her promise.

Shannon sent Victoria home with training tools, a schedule of appointments, and a dictate to get an X-pen, which is a thirty-inch-high wire pen, to keep Sidney from destroying the yard and house while Victoria worked.

"Shannon shows me this short pen called an X-pen, and I'm thinking, how the heck is this going to work? I've watched him jump over the back of my sofa, so I'm guessing if he wants out of this thing, it's going to happen. But he stayed put. Maybe he knew that he could get out of it if he wanted to and that calmed him. Whatever the reason was, it was the only thing that allowed me to get any work done."

"When did you know it was going to work out for you two?" I asked.

"About six weeks into our journey, I fell asleep in front of the TV and hadn't put him in the X-pen. When I woke up on the sofa and he hadn't destroyed the house while I slept, I knew I could begin to trust him. But I also remember a day three days into our partnership. We were playing tug of war. I tugged and got the toy away from him and turned to run. He lunged for it and got my arm instead. He immediately released my arm and jumped back. He was so sorry and contrite. I knew then that we'd already bonded."

I asked her if she knew much about Sidney's previous situation. And she replied that he had been purchased as a puppy. The parents divorced, and when the kids begged for a puppy, the father was all too willing to placate the kids with whatever they wanted, and they bought Sidney. Inevitably, the kids quickly got bored and Sidney spent his days alone in the backyard.

"They basically put him out at 7:00 a.m. when they woke up and brought him back in to go in his crate around 11:00 p.m. when they were ready to go to bed. They did nothing with him in the way of training or playing. He spent his days playing alone in the backyard with a ball. He'd play soccer, kicking and then chasing the ball. He's still a very good soccer player, but now he kicks the ball to me."

No wonder he's so ball crazy, I thought. Like Wilson, the volleyball Tom Hanks branded with his hand and bonded with so deeply in the movie *Castaway*, balls had been the only friend Sidney had ever known.

"The family would take a nightly walk around the neighborhood," she continued. "But they never took him. Although, considering all the paraphernalia he came with— leashes, all sorts of collars, even a harness—they might have tried to take him at first. He was horrible on a leash with me in the beginning."

Sidney and Victoria adopted a structured training regime, reinforcing what they learned during their sessions with Shannon, whose methods consist of rigidly precise choreographed drills.

"The key was teaching Sidney that, no matter what was going on around him, he had to stay focused on me," she said. "It was critical that he pay attention. We worked for an hour and a half a day. Walking and working. And we loved it. It took about six weeks, but Sidney blossomed into this amazing dog, and I could tell that he loved our work. He loved his job and knowing that I had expectations of him."

When Sidney had been with her for fifteen months, Victoria began to consider getting another dog. So she reached out to Shannon for advice. Shannon's response was immediate. She loved the idea but stressed that the new dog needed to be a female.

Victoria contacted the German Shepherd rescue that she and I eventually both began volunteering for, scheduled a meet-and-greet with two females that had appealed to her on the website, and set off with Sidney.

A volunteer met them at the boarding facility the rescue used for dogs who didn't have foster homes. The volunteer stood in the front yard with the first female in tow. Victoria clipped a leash on Sidney's collar and brought him from her car. The female curled her lip at Sidney before they were even close to one another. It was a clear "no." The second female Victoria had been interested in had already been adopted, so the volunteer suggested another. A large, fluffy, black and tan Shepherd named Hannah. Victoria agreed to meet Hannah, so the volunteer entered the boarding enclosure and returned with Hannah. And Victoria and the volunteer began to walk the dogs. Sidney was immediately comfortable in Hannah's presence, and the two walked calmly side by side as if they had known each other for years. It was a clear "yes."

Victoria loaded both dogs in the back of her SUV and headed home.

"About halfway home, I panicked, realizing that I essentially had two huge dogs riding free in the back of my car who were strangers and had only spent about thirty minutes together. And there was no guarantee that they wouldn't go at each other if something set them off. So I moved into the slow lane on the freeway in case I had to pull over to separate them."

But there was no fight. Hannah moved in, and the two transitioned peacefully, becoming best friends.

But even in Hannah's calming presence, Sidney continued to be a prankster. Once he broke into a visitor's purse, claiming her prescription for Xanax, crunching the vial open and strewing the contents on the floor. Luckily, there had been only two pills left, and Victoria retrieved them before Sidney could.

One night when I joined them for dinner, I left my paper napkin unattended. Sidney gingerly stole it from my lap, backing stealthily away from the table as though if he moved slowly enough we wouldn't see him. Victoria snatched it from his teeth. Moments later, we heard crunching sounds. Sidney had dragged my purse from the sofa, nosed his way through the pockets, and was mangling my sunglasses.

When guests stay for a visit, Sidney will often sneak into their bedroom or bathroom to investigate their belongings to see if there is anything he needs to "borrow."

"He's especially intent on stealing things from guests he feels aren't giving him enough attention," Victoria said, chuckling. "I had two friends visiting once. One lavished attention on Sidney. The other wasn't really a dog person, so she paid less attention to Sidney. Sidney snuck into the guest bathroom and stole the toothbrush of the guest who'd been ignoring him. I don't know how he knew which toothbrush was the right one, probably it was the scent, but it was comical. I stock extra toothbrushes now."

One day, Victoria turned her back on him and he jumped on the kitchen counter with his front paws and grabbed a butcher knife, plucking it from the dish drainer by its handle, and then ran around the house like a maniac with the knife in his mouth.

"I couldn't chase him," she said. "That would have just made it like a game to him. And I didn't want to try to grab the knife in my hands anyway, so I just had to act like I wasn't interested, and he quickly dropped it when he realized he wouldn't get a reaction from me. Then there was the time I'd unwittingly left my IRS refund check out and he snatched it. That time, I did chase him. Getting the IRS to issue a duplicate check would have been such a nuisance."

One day just before Christmas, Victoria emailed me, requesting that I ask Sidney why he had eaten his Santa hat.

I tuned into him and said, "Did you eat your Santa?"

Don't be ridiculous.

I laughed. Such a droll personality. "Vic says you ate him."

No response.

"Well?"

He was tasty.

To this day, Victoria still can't leave paper lying around. So her mail is hidden in her desk, toilet paper is carefully stashed in a closed cupboard, and paper napkins have been replaced by fabric.

When he was five, Sidney developed symmetrical lupoid onychodystrophy/onychitis (SLO), a disease in which the dog's antibodies begin to attack the toenails. It's an uncommon and painful disease that causes the nails to fall off. For weeks, Sidney was on a regimen of antibiotics and now takes vitamin E and niacinamide to keep it from reoccurring. Healing took months, but despite the veterinarian's mandate that he refrain from ball time, Sidney wasn't having it. At about 2:45 each day, he'd sit near Victoria while she worked and vocalize that it was time they go outside to play. Victoria toned down their routine to keep his movement to a minimum, kicking the ball gingerly so it didn't go far.

"I knew it had to be uncomfortable for him," she said. "But he didn't care. The joy he got from our playtime almost seemed to mask the pain. But he wasn't allowed to run around like a crazy man after the ball. I would barely tap the ball with my toe, sending it rolling slowly not much more than a foot or so away from me. And as soon as I kicked it, he pounced and claimed his prize. With the ball in his jaws, he'd won. That's what he cared about."

When he was nine, Victoria began to notice a slight decline in the quality of movement in his hind end. She and her vet decided upon two tests. The first was a set of X-rays; the second, a blood test to determine whether the cause was degenerative myelopathy (DM), a progressive disease of the spinal cord. The disease has an insidious onset typically between eight and fourteen years of age. It begins with a loss of coordination in the hind limbs. The affected dog will wobble when walking and, as the disease progresses, lose function of the back legs.

To complicate things, DM can only be clearly diagnosed after a dog has passed away, via an autopsy. So the only option is to test for the possibility of DM by manipulating the limbs and looking at the results of the bloodwork. If a dog carries the possibility of DM, it shows up through the presence of mutated genes in the DNA. No mutated genes means the dog doesn't have DM. One mutated gene means the dog can be a carrier of DM. Two mutated genes means the dog is at risk. Sidney's tests revealed he had one mutated gene but didn't confirm that he had the disease.

However, the X-rays revealed that he had a swollen disc at the base of his tail, and the vet recommended surgery to remove it. But the surgery meant six weeks of crate rest. Then, almost at the end of his recovery, he slipped in the house and reinjured himself, which meant four more weeks of crate time.

"I had bought the largest crate I could find so he could at least stand at times," she said.

The surgery appeared to be a success, and for a while Sidney seemed to have improved. But eventually he began to decline again. Since X-rays ruled out hip dysplasia, this time the vet was more confident that Sidney had DM. Victoria tried assorted remedies to keep him healthy and the disease at bay. They experimented with stem cell replacement, cold laser therapy, acupuncture, and chiropractic work.

One of the treatments Victoria tried was swim therapy. She'd drive Sidney to a facility about twenty minutes from her home. They'd place him in a clear-glass tank where he could stand on a treadmill. Then they filled the tank with water up to his chest. The theory was that, buoyed by the water, Sidney could exercise without injuring himself. It was only a theory. Sidney disliked it at first and then began to hate it. It got to the point that he would begin to rear and buck like a horse, defeating the entire purpose of the therapy. After four or five attempts, Victoria and the therapist agreed that the treatment was doing more harm than good, and Sidney got his way.

Victoria doesn't know which of the therapies she tried was the most effective, but now, years later, her vet believes that the fact Sidney's issues haven't escalated more rapidly and that he's still relatively mobile at the age of thirteen is nothing short of a miracle. Most dogs with DM last a year at the most. And her advice to other dog owners with the same problem is to try everything you have available.

While Sidney is beginning to show his age, he's still a stunning and basically healthy dog. Part of that is the balanced diet Victoria feeds him. He eats better than some humans, consuming a diet of organic chicken, apples, sweet potatoes, broccoli, parsley, and turmeric, warmed on the stove and mixed with kibble. And he takes vitamin E, fish oil, and glucosamine chondroitin to keep him in optimal health. His diet, supplements, daily ball-time regimen, and exercises to help strengthen his hip muscles keep him as fit and healthy as he can be.

I asked Victoria what it meant to her to have Sidney in her life.

"He's my rock," she said. "And he's my rock star. He's always so concerned about me. He's stunning. He's a showstopper. He's the essence of tall, dark, and handsome. He's steady, stable, good-natured, and smart. He's good with everyone he meets, human and canine. He's the man every woman dreams about."

She went on to say that Sidney makes her feel so safe. Although he's allowed to sleep on the bed, he never has. Instead, he sleeps between her bed and the door every night, barricading the space should an intruder ever make it that far into the house. He's just so in love with her.

I asked her what Sidney had taught her. "So much," she said, "but two key things come to mind. The first is that if you devote time to training and communication, you'll never imagine what you'll get back. He's incredible. He's the perfect companion. The second is that, as partners, dogs can be so much better than men. Dogs are so sincere and honest and transparent. They don't have egos or hidden agendas. They are simply the essence of goodness and kindness."

Next, I asked what her life would have been like had Sidney not been a part of it.

"I would have mourned forever," she said, tearing up. "So much time would have been spent grieving Newt's death. Sidney lifted me out of that. Out of my depression. He helped me heal. He healed me. He saved me from myself and my misery."

Looking for another piece of their story, I grabbed my friend Jill's *Geometries of Creation* card deck and asked for a message about Sidney and Victoria. The card I pulled was titled Complementary Relationship. Its meaning is that sometimes we encounter people or situations or ideas that can seem or feel contrary to what we think we want in our lives because, in reality, we are not seeing them for who or what they truly are. And I understood the message. That we sometimes misjudge people. And later, in coming to know them, their true beauty is revealed. It was this way for Victoria in the beginning. She wasn't sure she wanted Sidney. She didn't recognize his beauty. Until she came to know him and he won her heart.

After our interview, I connected with Sidney and I asked him to tell me about his relationship with Victoria.

She makes me her world. I feel that I am the center of her universe. I know how diligently she works to make sure I have the best of everything. She helps me realize my ultimate potential. And then I get to share that with everyone I meet.

"What do you think you do for her?"

I keep things light. I am a comedian. But I also keep her balanced. Like making sure we do ball time.

"Isn't ball time more for you than her?"

No. She'd work too much if it wasn't for me.

"I believe that there is a purpose for every human-animal partnership. Do you know what yours is with Victoria?

I help her manifest. I do this by helping her be grounded and balanced like I said earlier. As you suggested, we were meant to be.

Then he showed me a picture of a figure skater gliding on the ice, gracefully carving a figure 8 into a frozen pond. The infinity symbol. What was so striking to me about this vision was that it so beautifully represents him. Sidney's power and grace is reflected in the fluidity and strength of the figure skater. This is how Victoria sees him. And the infinity symbol reflects the eternal bond they share. They will live in each other's hearts forever.

Lizzy and Jill

When her husband left on an errand and returned with a rotund black Labrador Retriever puppy in his arms, she had no idea this dog would help her manifest her life's work.

"I remember it so clearly," Jill said. "My son and I were arguing, as usual, about my need for him to clean his room. We stood on the stairs, he two steps above me, bickering like magpies, and in walks my husband, Esty, with the most adorable little creature we'd ever seen. Of course, my son and I both melted into a puddle of oohs and aahs, and the fight was over."

They named her Lizzy. An unconscious choice that Jill later realized might have been fated. Jill is an intuitive spiritual counselor, and she uses many modalities in her work. One of them is a system called numerology, wherein each letter of the alphabet has a numeric value that equates to specific personality traits connected to our physical, mental/ emotional, and spiritual selves. To determine Lizzie's numbers, Jill assigned the appropriate number to each vowel and consonant in Lizzie's name and then added them together to get a separate number to describe the dog's physical, mental/ emotional, and spiritual essence.

When she was done, she learned that both she and Lizzy were a 1-7-8 combination. On a spiritual level, they were both original, pioneering, and leaders. On a mental level, they were wise, mystical, and exploratory. On a physical level, they were powerful, manifesting, and ambitious. It was as though they shared the same energetic DNA.

I'd known Jill for years. She has been an important mentor in my journey toward becoming able to communicate with animals. In time, she became a dear and trusted friend, helping me to navigate my life in ways I'd never imagined and helping me to understand issues I faced on a deeper level. She once told me that Lizzy had been instrumental in helping her to manifest and create her book and card deck *Geometries of Creation*. And one day, I asked her to tell me more about their story.

"Lizzy was born on my golden birthday. The year you turn the same age as the day of your birthday. Lizzy was born on September 27, and I was 27 when she entered my life."

Jill and her husband had agreed not to have another dog. They already had cats and were a busy family constantly on the go. Both Jill and her husband worked out of the house full-time, and their son wasn't home much. Not a situation they'd want for a dog. But all that changed when Esty walked in with Lizzy. Jill plucked the little dog from Esty's arms, melted into her plump, warm puppy body, and fell in love. Lizzy became their world, and they adored her.

Lizzy was part Lab, part Greyhound. Slender and refined with delicate feet, a show-stopping ebony coat that hugged her frame, and a curious snout she'd use to investigate guests' crotches.

"It was as embarrassing as it was funny. We'd warn people when they walked through the door, but there she was, nudging people's privates with that nose of hers. Boink boink boink. And she'd pinch sometimes…ever so slightly… with her teeth. Once my uncle was visiting, and he sprawled in an easy chair, legs spread-eagle. Lizzy approached him, and I warned him to close his legs. He waved me off, unconcerned. Lizzy zeroed in on his manhood and pinched him. He was more careful after that."

Upbeat, pleasant, and mellow, she integrated with the family easily. She hated fetch but loved tug of war with socks or rubber rings. Lizzy was a typical Libra. Airy, affable, happy-go-lucky, and always aware of the balance that was needed. Libras are communicators and like to do everything with a partner. Which made her partnership with Jill all the more understandable.

It was interesting to me that both Martha and Jill connected their dogs' personality traits to an astrological sign. Before interviewing Martha and Jill for this book, I'd never considered that animals might take on the astrological qualities of their birthday. They opened my eyes in regard to that and made me wish I knew my horse's birthday. It might explain a lot.

Like Jill, Lizzy was a total foodie, and she inherited Jill's love of sweets and Cheetos. If food was involved, she was a master at devising ways to get at it. In fact, the only foods she refused to eat were liver sausage and lettuce. So Jill was diligent in respect to making sure her dog didn't get into something she wasn't supposed to.

"Her favorite thing was to follow toddlers around. Two-year-olds whose heads were the same height as she. She'd snatch food daintily from their hands. When we had guests, I had to tell them not to leave food in their rooms or Lizzy would find it. She was constantly stealing food my son had left in his room."

On one occasion, a guest left a tin of sugar cookies under the bed. The door was ajar, so Lizzy pushed it open with her nose, wriggled under the six-inch space below the bed, opened the tin with her teeth, and devoured three dozen cookies. When another guest left a chocolate bar in her unmonitored purse, Lizzy sniffed it out, stole it from the inner pocket, and chomped half of it before Jill heard her and took it away. She ate Jill's nephew's Halloween candy and got into a guest's blood pressure medicine. Luckily, there were only two tablets, and a frantic call to the vet revealed that Lizzy would be fine and likely just spend a very chill afternoon sleeping.

"One day, my niece and I were walking up the stairs to visit in my sitting room. We each carried a chocolate éclair. I started to tell her to be careful that Lizzy didn't snatch her éclair when Lizzy spun and gobbled mine," she said, giggling.

"I wonder about something," I said. "It's interesting that you and Lizzy were such foodies. Channeling energy the way you do is draining, exhausting work. You have to refuel. When I was involved with dog rescue, I would come home after an event and eat nonstop. I know I was channeling and communicating with the dogs. Maybe that's how you both had to replenish."

Like a toddler just learning to talk, Lizzy loved the sound of her own voice. And she vocalized constantly, barking and howling at anything she saw outside that moved. Jill worried that the neighbors would be annoyed. She taught her to growl instead by placing her hands softly around Lizzy's muzzle and growling. Soon Lizzy took the cue, and instead of barking, she'd wander window to window growling like a bear.

And like many dogs, Lizzy had quite the sense of smell. Jill felt she would have made a fantastic drug-detection dog. The only two people who had come to visit that Lizzy took offense to were both drug users, and she backed each up the stairs hackles up, eyes wild, a menacing growl uncoiling from her throat. Jill said she didn't know about the drugs at the time. It was something she discovered later. Then she made the connection to Lizzy's scent detection. The dog knew something was off.

"Lizzy oozed love," Jill said, "but I think that's true of all dogs. What I've come to understand through the research I did for my book is that each species is connected to a dimension. We live in a three-dimensional world, but there are many dimensions available to us beyond that, each with specific properties like self-identification, magnetism, reasoning, translation, etc."

Jill went on to explain that dimensions form triads and each triad is connected via a portal. Our collective human race is in the process of transitioning or evolving beyond the third-dimensional reality we live in. The fourth dimension is actually a portal within us that allows us to access the fifth dimension. Fourth dimension is all about love.

Unconditional love. It's heart energy. Dogs are connected to the fourth dimension. And as a collective consciousness, they are a vehicle for helping the human race to access their hearts and evolve.

"The more I came to understand this system," she said, "the more I saw that the properties of fourth dimension were so accurately portrayed by dogs. As a species, they love us so unconditionally. They are totally tuned into us spiritually. They are a dimensional bridge that nurtures our fourth dimensional reality into existence. They are essentially pulling us into the fourth dimension so we can evolve. They give us their lives. No matter what happens, they still love us."

Lizzy came into Jill's life in 1978, the year she started studying metaphysics. During that time, the two became deeply connected. And although she was the family's companion, she became Jill's dog.

"Lizzy was glued to me unless my son had food," Jill said and laughed. "And I quickly realized I had a telepathic bond with her. I would think something, and she'd get it."

"How did you see that? I mean, how did that manifest?" I asked.

"Like if I was thinking about what I should make for dinner, I'd find her sitting in front of the fridge staring at it. Or if I was thinking about taking out the trash, I'd find her by the trash can, and once I grabbed it, she'd head to the door. If I planned to take her for a walk, I had to block it from my mind or she would have been all over me until we left."

Jill was introduced to an important teacher in 1978 who trained her to use telepathy, communicating with the mind to tap into her spiritual teachers and guardian angels. Her quest began when her then nine-year-old son ran into her office and said, "Mom I just figured something out. You know that feeling when you're just about to fall asleep and then something jerks you awake? It's your spirit jumping back into your body!"

His exclamation triggered a spark in her and sent her on a personal quest about expanding consciousness. She attended classes, workshops, and lectures; read books on astrology, parapsychology, and metaphysics; and was fueled by an insatiable thirst for knowledge. She practiced tuning into and receiving information from her guides.

One day during a meditation, she received a message that our human energy centers, or chakras, are not locked into form but rather working interconnectedly with and through each other. With each following meditation, she was shown pictures and shapes morphing from one state to another, each with a message, each linked to a dimension she was instructed to unlock and translate. Every day, she worked with her guides, channeling the information on a new dimension. Until all sixty-four had been unlocked, decoded, and identified.

When she was done, she began to create a deck of cards. One for each dimension and each with an explanation of the properties connected to it. The deck was black and white, allowing the user to physically color the card and bring the properties of the dimensions into their cellular bodies for use. Each card had a different meaning and purpose. Some held healing energy to be harnessed. Others creativity. Still others represented purpose, destiny, and compassion.

"It was a wonderful, magical experience. But it took a toll on my physical body. The pictures my guides showed me were three-dimensional, holographic, moving shapes. It was almost impossible for me to capture them on paper because they morphed. Sometimes I'd grab my head and scream, 'You've got to make the shapes stay still.' Then my guides would slow or stop the movement so I could capture it in rough form and channel the rest of the message."

Jill's first metaphysics teacher had taught her to "keep an open mind; just don't let your brain fall out." It was the basis for helping her to understand the importance of grounding oneself during the process of tapping into other creatures and realms.

Lizzy was by Jill's side while she worked, lying at Jill's feet while she documented what she'd been shown, made rough drawings of the images, and captured the information she'd been given into a book.

"I realized later that Lizzy was helping me with the process of creating the deck and the book. She made sure I was grounded so the information I was processing didn't damage my body. I was told in a meditation that if I hadn't been grounded, the energy I was channeling was so intense and so foreign to my physical form that I could have fried myself."

She paused and then continued. "Lizzy made sure I was physically and spiritually safe while I channeled this information and pulled it through. If she hadn't been with me, I couldn't have seen the shapes or given them form. When she was with me, it just flowed. If she left to get a drink, I was totally blocked. She was the mechanism for my ability to channel."

Jill formally published *Geometries of Creation* in 1994, six years after she'd begun the channeling process. Lizzie passed away soon after. She'd come into Jill's life at the beginning of her metaphysical journey, and she crossed over when *Geometries of Creation* had been birthed. Her passing also happened soon after Jill had taught her first class on dealing with death and dying.

"When Lizzy was twelve," Jill said, "I knew she had three years left. I told her that it was coming but that she and I would get through it together. I made her promise me that, when the time came, she had to find a way to get out of her body. To find a way to do it on her own. I'd been in the situation before and since of having to make the decision to euthanize a companion animal. But I told her that I couldn't be the one to end her life."

Near the end of her fifteenth year, Lizzy slowed down dramatically. She was stiff and achy. She had trouble digesting food and would sometimes vomit. She began losing control of her bowels and defecated in her bed. One day, Jill knew the end was near. They rushed her to the vet, and she collapsed in the waiting area.

"When she collapsed, I could feel her spirit leave her body. By the time we got her on the table, she was gone. I was at peace with her decision. But in her absence, the house was so quiet. So painfully quiet."

"How long did it take to adjust?" I asked.

She didn't answer right away, and I wondered if the phone line had gone dead.

"I still haven't," she said finally. Her voice on the other end of the line went quiet again. I could feel her pain, and I began to cry. When she spoke again, her voice was husky with emotion. "Twenty years later, and I still feel the pain. She was always there. It's so intense when you can't access them. I was devastated. It was like losing a part of myself."

Jill said she thought she may have manifested Lizzy into her life to help her channel the work she needed to accomplish, that she manifested Lizzy to be a part of her energetic being to assist in doing what Jill couldn't do herself. She felt that, in a metaphysical sense, she and Lizzy were the same person. Like twins who shared a secret language or a special communication. And when one leaves, the other is lost. Lizzy was Jill's canine soulmate.

"What would you say to her if she walked through your door right now?"

"I wouldn't say anything. I'd just hug her. She'd probably ask me if she had more work to do." We laughed through our tears.

"What would your life have been like if she hadn't been a part of it?" I asked.

"Empty. I would have lived in a vacuum, never experiencing any of this. I would have never accomplished my life's purpose."

"What did you do for her?" I asked.

"I gave her the best life I could. Love. Play. Exercise. Companionship. I met her needs and gave her what she gave to me." She paused for a moment, as if remembering every moment of the fifteen years she spent with her beloved dog, and then continued. "Those were the days of magic and miracles," Jill said, remembering the years with Lizzy. "She was magic and miracles."

I asked Jill what she thought Lizzy had taught her, and she replied that she'd come to a different level of awareness in regard to the creatures we call pets. She'd learned that they are sentient beings, as evolved as, if not more than, humans. That they have the ability to communicate and the capacity to coexist with a form of communication that isn't a language but an unspoken awareness.

When I asked Lizzy what being with Jill had meant to her, she showed me a picture of a large, golden sun warming the earth with long, gentle rays that stretched from Heaven to the ground. Then a rainbow hung with ten winged hearts spanning edge to edge over an immense ocean of blue-green waves. Just before her energy receded, I heard her whisper a message for Jill. Just two simple words.

Thank you.

Jill believes that, because of the immense importance of what Lizzy helped her manifest, Lizzy added to the canine gene pool and to their existence, which allowed all dogs to have better connections with their humans. She believes that Lizzy helped humans and animals evolve. And she believes that this beautiful dog took an evolutionary step for all who met her and went away changed.

Jill's book is dedicated to Lizzy. With thanks. And from the depths of her heart.

To learn more about Jill and her work, to book a reading, or to purchase *Geometries of Creation*, email her at intuvision@roadrunner.com.

Rayne and Carol

"From the moment I met her, I knew I had to take her. I connected with her immediately, more so than with any other dog I'd met. I've been around dogs all my life, but I felt so at peace with her. And I knew I had to save her."

Rayne is a Czechoslovakian Shepherd with a short, wiry, silver and black coat and high-energy, intense eyes framed by arched, silver eyebrows. She was relinquished by her people to Shepherds Hope Rescue. The dad worked all day, and the mom couldn't handle Rayne's energy, so prior to her rescue, Rayne had spent her days tied to a tree.

Rayne was one of the special dogs Carol took on to train in drug and bomb detection work through her own rescue.

"We call them throw-away dogs," she said. "Their people drop them off at our pet hotel and then never return for them. I mean, what kind of heartless person does that? Shows up with their dog, knowingly gives us a fake name, pays cash for the stay, and then disappears. That's why I started my rescue. And then it morphed into more. Before I knew it, I was rescuing dogs who had the potential to do police work and donating them to police departments that otherwise couldn't afford them. I met Rayne. And that's when my life really changed."

Carol is the PR and Marketing Rep for a pet hotel located in the Philadelphia area. It's a high-end resort for dogs. Their primary service is to provide a fabulous stay for dogs whose people are on vacation.

"It's the perfect job for me," Carol said. "I used to work for a vet, and that was often sad. Animals came in scared or sick or both. Sometimes, they had to be euthanized. But at the hotel, all the dogs are happy and healthy, and they're going home, so they make me happy. The only negative aspect is when their family doesn't return for them."

When that happens, staff members foster the dog until a suitable home can be found. Carol often does much of the networking. The left-behind dogs always find homes but not without the entire ordeal taking an emotional toll on Carol and other staff.

"I got so angry about what was happening that one day that I wrote a rant in our company newsletter titled 'How Did Your Throw-Away Dog Rescue You?' People who'd adopted our 'throw-away dogs' were invited to share a picture and a story for a chance to be in our annual calendar. Many people submitted stories and photos. Others donated things we needed. It was wildly successful. And we actually sold enough calendars to donate a year's worth of dog food to New Leash on Life dog rescue."

The cover dog was Winchester, a stunning, 120-pound, sable male German Shepherd who'd been relinquished by his people when they became overwhelmed by his high-energy temperament. Winchester was saved from impending euthanasia and sent to Philadelphia, where he was paired with his current human partner, Officer Jason Walters, a policeman who trained him to be a working police dog and eventually his K9 partner.

Jason often boarded his dogs where Carol worked, and the two began talking about the crisis the boarding facility faced with the left-behind dogs. So they teamed to create the calendar. When the calendar was so wildly successful, Carol and Jason decided to create Throw Away Dogs Project, a nonprofit 501(c)(3) organization that locates unwanted shelter dogs and trains them to become working police dogs used primarily for detecting bombs and drugs. And they hoped that future calendars could become a source of fundraising for their new nonprofit.

"So often, it's the high-energy, high-strung dogs who are relinquished. For us, that's a positive. We look for energy and drive because these dogs thrive in training, and their job is like playtime for them, their time to play hide and seek. So often though, people don't want such a high-drive dog. They're not seen as adoptable. We take these high-drive, sometimes-difficult dogs and give them a second chance."

Carol explained that the training process is an expensive one, but it's a gift to everyone. To Carol and her business partner, Jason. To the dogs. And to the police departments that could never afford them.

"Not every dog we pull from a shelter will make it through K9 school. When that happens, we are determined to find a loving home that will treat the dog like a valued and loved family member. No matter what these dogs end up doing, it's all important, whether they are serving as a K9 officer or a loving family member," Carol said. "The ones who don't make it through school...well, they'll just wear a different type of badge."

Once paired with Rayne, Carol boarded her at the pet hotel with the intention of training her. But the trainer who was originally set up to train Rayne didn't work out. So Carol worked on Rayne's basic obedience while she was at work and looked for another trainer.

"It killed me to leave her in the kennels, but my husband had made me promise: no more dogs. We already had three. But this wasn't what I wanted for her. I wanted her to be worked and socialized by a pro, not stuck in a kennel waiting for me to spend time with her. Despite my promise to my husband, I couldn't stand the current situation. So I brought her home."

At home, Carol learned that integrating Rayne into her existing pack wouldn't be easy. The dogs didn't get along. So they kept the dogs separated, carefully rotating them in and out of different rooms fenced off by baby gates so the dogs could see each other and get used to one another without physically being in the same space.

"It didn't always stop them from breaking down the barriers and tussling," Carol said. "Rayne thought she could come in and take over alpha status, and my dogs weren't having that. The baby gates were more of a reminder for my kids to be careful going from one room to another. We had to have a system. We couldn't make mistakes."

Carol's bond with Rayne deepened. In Rayne, she had a second shadow. Even human potty breaks weren't private now, and when Carol emerged from the shower, Rayne was always seated or lying down concealing the bathmat with her chiseled body. Often, when Carol readied herself for work, Rayne would open vanity doors, retrieving and opening plastic bags filled with cotton balls with her teeth. When Carol placed the bag back in the drawer, Rayne would have it out again just moments later.

"When she smelled something she wanted, she had to have it," Carol said. "That's when I knew she was going to make an awesome scent-detection dog."

She proved to be great with Carol's three children and a kind family companion, but she also displayed the immense drive, nose, and energy suited for detection work. Carol has always had a deep love for dogs and considered herself relatively knowledgeable. But Rayne's keen intelligence, drive, and tireless energy tested the boundaries of Carol's previous experience. None of her dogs had ever been as high energy as Rayne, so she had to learn to deal with and direct the sensitive dog.

"It did make me understand what causes people who aren't equipped to surrender a high-energy dog. I had to learn and grow and evolve. I almost gave up. The stress caused a ton of friction between my husband and me. But I couldn't give up on her. I'd fallen in love with her. And that's how we bonded. Through work. She made me better. And once I learned how to be her leader, she was like a normal dog. The more time I spent with her, the more amazing she proved herself to be. She was great with the kids. And she was selective with people, but for me, well, I could do anything with her. Clean her teeth and ears, and handle her paws. She was putty in my hands."

Within weeks of bringing Rayne home, Carol was contacted by a retired K9 handler who had heard of Carol's struggle. He offered to help her with Rayne. He lived ninety minutes away, and training sessions lasted two hours. So training days were a five-hour ordeal for Carol. And Rayne's energy level and anxiety issues caused her to chase cars while riding in a car. Spinning and barking and racing in the back seat. But they made bi-weekly treks to his property, and he worked with Rayne, training her in basic commands, such as recall, and enhancing her scent work. The trainer also worked with Carol so she could keep up the training on days they weren't with him. One of Carol's assignments was to work on reducing Rayne's anxiety level so she could focus on what was being asked of her.

Carol believes that the anxiety developed in her previous home where, tied to a tree, Rayne would bark at cars, squirrels, and birds. Later, this manifested in Rayne chasing cars, on leash or while riding in a vehicle.

"We finally got this under control so that, even when she was off leash and a car passed, we could verbally talk her through it. You could see she wanted to run and chase the cars, but she calmed herself down by doing one spin and a jump. It was weird, but it was her routine. And it was the routine that would break her anxiety cycle. She just needed a reminder, and I always kept up on it. In the car, I would talk to her and remind her that it was OK. Sometimes it didn't work and she would bark, but most of the time she controlled herself."

"What do you look for when you're evaluating dogs for detection temperament?" I asked.

"We look for an inquisitive dog, one with a desire to explore the environment. You want a dog that is a sniffer. High energy. High play drive and prey drive for retrieving, an apparent interest in odors, and highly responsive to treat/ reward interaction as well as to people," she said.

"And how do you approach training? How did the trainer start off with Rayne and develop her through the process?" I asked.

"At first, it was just basic obedience, like hold or place and recall, things like that. Then the dog is introduced to the scent of a bomb. Generally, hexachloroethane paired with a treat. Over time, the dog associates the scent with a treat, so they may salivate or wag their tail or show some physical sign associated with the treat," she said.

Carol's goal was to complete Rayne's training as an explosives dog and find a handler who would make her part of the family. With her initial training completed, Carol found someone she thought would be ideal. But Rayne was returned five days later. The handler had decided to play fetch with Rayne and his other dog off leash. It hadn't gone well.

"Wait…two strange dogs…off leash…with a toy involved? Who does that?" I asked.

"I know. That just set her up for failure."

So Carol continued to work with her and found that the more love she lavished on the special dog, the more Rayne wanted to please her. Rayne had become part of a family. Probably for the first time in her life.

Carol will tell you that Rayne is her inspiration for continuing the rescue efforts, despite the hard work, long hours, expense, rejection, and tedious drives back and forth from Philadelphia to New York to rescue dogs and to other locations to place dogs or get them to training.

"I had no idea how hard this would be," she said, "setting up and maintaining a rescue. Nor did I foresee the roadblocks we'd face. The brick walls we'd slam into. The constant need to raise money."

Carol is grateful to have Jason as a partner in their organization, as Jason, being a seasoned K9 Law Enforcement Officer, can often open doors that Carol can't. They complement each other and work well together.

"As long as I'm saving dogs, I can deal with egos of people who think they know it all," Carol said. "That's why

I'm in this. Right now, we're primarily looking for and placing scent dogs, but we want to expand into therapy dogs and search and rescue. But we need a sponsor. Because at the moment, it's just Jason and me."

Since Throw Away Dogs doesn't charge adoption fees, raising funds is even more paramount to their success. Their rescue asks only for an invitation to the graduation ceremony and a photo of the dog and handler.

Four weeks after Rayne's return, a woman contacted Carol through the social media vehicle Twitter. She had a lead on a new training facility. Carol called them, and they agreed to evaluate Rayne. The handler was an officer for the Maryland Police Department, and they were looking for a narcotics dog. So Carol crated Rayne, loaded her in the car, and made the three-hour trek. When they arrived, the handler put Rayne through her paces, hiding toys in the tall field grass for her to seek and retrieve. Rayne passed every test he asked of her. But this was more than just an opportunity to work. Rayne would be welcomed into the family, and she'd have children to watch over. The only catch was that the family wasn't ready for Rayne for three more weeks. When they were, Carol delivered Rayne back to them, where Rayne would start the three-month training process of identifying the scents of different drugs.

"I cried like a baby as soon as I saw them," Carol told me. "I knew and felt they were good people, and this was going to be a perfect match for her. Rayne deserved this. It's the strangest thing," Carol said, her voice cracking as she spoke, "to relinquish a dog to an ideal situation, the very thing they are suited for, the very things you've dreamt for them, while your heart is being shredded. I knew I had to give her up, to allow her to fulfill her destiny. But it was bittersweet. I loved that dog more than you can imagine. But I learned from her that I can't give up on my dream of building this rescue. This journey isn't easy, but they're worth it. The dogs are worth it. They have hearts, and souls, and desires. If I had given up, Rayne would have been done."

When Carol and I were done with our interview, I tuned into Rayne and asked her what her time with Carol had meant to her.

She saved my life. She showed me the way.

"How do you feel about your work and life now? Do you like detection work?"

It's an honor. I know it's important work.

"How do you know?"

My handlers. I watch their reactions. I can see it in their eyes. In how they praise me.

"You're defending our country, you know. Your work keeps us safe. It *is* important. You just needed someone to believe in you. Have you adjusted to your new home?"

I have. But Carol will always be in my heart. She was the first person to love me.

"And you always remember your first," I said and smiled.

What?

"Stupid joke. It's something we humans say."

Mmmm.

After we talked, Carol sent me a video of Rayne compiled through a montage of still photos and short video clips. I watched Rayne running free through lush fields, recalling on command, retrieving sticks and what looked like boat bumpers, biting at water flowing from a hose. All set to Katy Perry's beautiful love song "Unconditionally." Tears filled my eyes and ran down my cheeks as I watched. It was a beautiful tribute to a beautiful dog and a beautiful relationship. I emailed Carol and told her how touching it was.

Thank you for sharing this, I wrote. *It's so powerful, I was moved to tears. The song says it all. Your unconditional love and belief in her saved her. I can't wait to tell your story. I will try to do you and your girl justice.*

Oh, my God, she wrote back, *now I'm crying. You called her my girl?*

She'll always be your girl, I responded.

Rayne's new handler kept in touch with Carol every few days. The plan was to allow her to be a family dog for two weeks prior to starting K9 school so she could bond and connect with her new human and canine family.

"I worried a bit," she confided, "because of the other dog and the situation that had occurred in New York. And I didn't want to bug them for information, but I was on pins and needles. Especially after what had supposedly happened in her last situation. But when I did follow up, they reported that there'd been no issues at all with her new human family as well as her new canine friend. They were falling in love with her and couldn't wait to start school."

Two weeks later, school started. Days passed, but Carol heard nothing. She waited anxiously and tried to be patient, trusting she would hear from them at some point. Three weeks into Rayne's training, Carol received a frantic text from the handler asking her to call him immediately.

"I freaked," she said. "My heart pounded, and my mind raced, wondering what the issue could be. When I spoke with him, my first question to him was, is she OK? I thought something happened to her."

Rayne was physically fine but had just failed K9 school. Her anxiety had resurfaced with a vengeance. And she barked uncontrollably in the car and at passing cars around her.

Carol had worked so hard with her and had gotten that problem under control, but the new handler drove one and half hours to the testing K9 facility and Rayne spun and barked the entire way. Once they arrived at school, she was drained and unwilling to work. The head trainer questioned Rayne's ability to spend the day in a patrol car and then actually work once they arrived at their destination.

"But you had this behavior under control?" I said.

"It was explained to me that every handler and owner is different," she said. "But if they don't reinforce things and continue to practice daily, the dogs will revert back to their bad habits."

Once again, Carol made a seven-hour drive round-trip to retrieve Rayne.

"I equated this process to a bad cold that wouldn't go away. Each time, I thought I had found a placement that would work for Rayne and be in her best interests. I began to doubt myself. I wondered if my love for Rayne was clouding my judgment about her skills. Was I seeing something that wasn't there? Was she truly not as talented as I thought she was?"

As the family hugged Rayne and kissed her goodbye, one of the handler's neighbors came over to say goodbye to her also. They were introduced, and the neighbor asked Carol, if this next "job" didn't work out, would she consider adopting her out to him?

"I almost fell to the floor. He said he and his family spent time with Rayne and they love her and would love to give her a home. He was a German Shepherd guy and had four other Shepherds at home. They live on a huge property with several acres with a fenced in yard. I expressed my concern about the other dogs, and he said that Rayne had already been introduced
to them several times and there were no issues."

She then faced the difficult decision of deciding upon Rayne's fate...again. Rayne had amazing working-dog qualities but had been bounced from home to home, from trainer to trainer and had traveled hours and hours in a car, which she ultimately hated.

So despite Rayne's potential, Carol made the decision to "retire" her and give her the opportunity to be a family dog with the neighbors who were experienced with high-energy dogs like Rayne. As time passed, Carol kept in touch with the family. They were falling in love. Rayne was settling in and was able to bond with her new family while keeping in touch with her old family across the street.

Ultimately, things didn't work out and Rayne was returned. Rayne and Carol picked up right where they left off. Their bond remained unchanged, and Carol still believed Rayne to be perfect in every way. It devastated her to know that, once again, they would have to part ways. A fact that tore at her heart.

"Rayne speaks to me with her eyes, and I wonder if she understands that I only want the best for her. I know she wants to stay with me, but it is not possible. As much as I love her, it creates so much stress for our family. But until then, it is my job to take care of her. That's my promise to her until I find her a forever home."

Almost a year later, another home surfaced. Carol messaged me on Facebook, shared the news, and then asked me if I could connect with Rayne and prepare her. She would meet her prospective family the next morning.

Her message read, *Tonight is my last night with Rayne. I take her tomorrow morning to her new home. I am sick to my stomach. Can you please try to connect with her? She is going to be devastated and not understand why she is being taken away from me again.*

I tuned into Rayne later that night.

"Rayne," I said focusing on her energy, "Carol has found you the perfect home. It will be an adjustment, but these are good people."

Why am I leaving?

"Because the situation with Carol isn't in anyone's best interests. You have to be sequestered in another room while Carol's dogs are out, or they have to be shut away when you are out. None of you get along. It's stressful for you, for the other dogs, for Carol. She loves you so much. But sometimes love alone isn't enough to keep the peace. Know that Carol loves you more than you can even imagine. Try to trust the process and these new people."

I understand. Will I see her again?

"I don't know. It will depend on whatever is in your best interests. Carol really believes this family is a match for you. But she loves you dearly, and this is killing her. She just doesn't want you to be bounced around anymore."

The next morning, Carol loaded Rayne into the car and made the long, emotional drive to Rayne's new family. She showed them Rayne's routine and went over the training exercises that would calm Rayne's agitation. When there was nothing more to say or do or teach, she knelt and took Rayne in her arms, holding her one last time. She then made her way to her car, eyes brimming with tears. She sat behind the wheel for a few minutes, crying, and then started the car and drove home. When she arrived, she messaged me again.

Thank you again, Dobie, for all your help. She is so special to me, and this is killing me. I want to keep her because no one loves her like I do. But it's not fair to my dogs or to her with all this rotation and them having to be locked in a bedroom while Rayne is out. And poor Rayne, she deserves to be the center of attention and the apple of someone's eye.

I replied back. *I know. You two are such a team. It's really so sad. I connected with her again last night and asked her to please give these people a chance.*

Two days later, I reached out to check on Carol. She hadn't heard from the family, Her stomach was still in knots, and she'd spent most of the past two days crying.

Three weeks later, Carol messaged me again. Rayne's family proclaimed that she was a handful, but they had found a trainer to work with them, and they were making progress with her, and everyone was settling into the new routine.

As I reflected on their story, I wondered what the purpose was behind Carol and Rayne coming into each other's lives. Clearly, Rayne needed someone with perseverance who wouldn't give up on her as so many others had. And Rayne had taught Carol much about partnering with and leading a high-energy, high-maintenance dog. But it was more than that. I think Carol and Rayne recognized themselves in each other. Two determined, spirited, independent females cut from the same cloth, a reflection of each other's strengths and self-expression. They were a mirror for each other.

Carol was Rayne's guardian angel for almost two years. In that time, she took a troubled, anxious dog and allowed her to become her very best self. Although I never asked her, I imagine that if Carol had just a few words to say to Rayne, her message would be simple: "I love you, and I will always be here for you."

The Throw Away Dogs Project is a nonprofit 501(c)(3) organization founded by Carol Skaziak and Jason Walters. Their mission is to rescue high-drive dogs, train them, and then donate them to K9 police departments that cannot afford one. To learn more, visit www.throwawaydogsproject.com.

Willow and Dobie

She trotted toward me with short, choppy steps, her luxurious fur undulating like an over-flounced petticoat. I'd always wanted to meet her, but during my previous attempts to pet her, she'd eluded me like a feather on the wind. Until today. I bent to pet her, and she reared, butting her head into my hand like a tiny goat. Willow was a cat at the ranch where I board my horse. Because she was mainly an indoor cat, I rarely saw her and had only admired her from afar.

A friend who also boarded her horse at the ranch watched her rubbing against me and circling me, begging for affection. She asked me if I would consider taking her. Willow's family had moved to a new ranch, but due to the ongoing construction at the new place and the lack of fencing, they'd left the cats at the old ranch until the new one was secure.

She was a stunning girl. Probably the most beautiful I'd ever seen. A long-haired tortoiseshell streaked with bronze and black and cream. Roundish and sturdy with tufted ears and paws, she was reminiscent of the Maine Coon breed.

"You should take her home," my friend said. "How can you leave her here when she obviously likes you so much?"

"Well I can't just *take* her," I said. "Her family is going to move her when the new ranch is ready."

But as I walked to the pasture where my horse was grazing, Willow followed me, meowing incessantly. After I entered the riding arena to get my horse, she climbed a nearby masonry wall to keep tabs on me. Her cries broke my heart, and I began to feel that I couldn't leave her. I sent the owner a text message, offering to foster her until they were ready to take her home. Willow's owner responded that I could certainly take Willow.

Although I didn't have a cat carrier in the car with me and essentially no way of restraining her safely in a vehicle, I felt a strange sense of urgency that there wasn't time to go home and get one. I felt that I had to transport her immediately. So I picked her up and put her in the back seat of my car and got in the driver's seat, wondering how she'd do riding free.

She immediately freaked, bouncing around the confines of the car, jumping on the dashboard and then under my feet and then back to the dashboard looking for an escape. I turned the key in the ignition and cranked the AC to cool the interior, and we sat as I spoke to her, explaining my intentions.

"Don't worry. I mean you no harm. You will be safe. You're only coming home with me until your family is ready for you."

Within a minute, she settled on the floormat underneath my legs, pressing herself against the front of the driver's seat and looking up at me. Occasionally, she panted but then resumed normal breathing. And although she was stressed, I could tell she had heard me. Once I felt she had really settled, I eased the car down the ranch driveway and headed home. She didn't move or make a sound during the drive to my house.

When we arrived, I carried her into the house and set her down. She poked curiously around the room and then sauntered down the hall, returning to rub against me and butt her head into my armpit, seemingly joyful about our new connection. I reiterated my message about her eventually being reunited with her family and then set up a litter box and dashed to town for food.

She gave me my first scare within days. I was sitting at my computer playing games when I heard a loud crash in the adjacent room. I sprang from my chair and dashed to the other room. The sliding screen door lay flat on the patio and she was in the backyard, lured by the birds she'd been watching. I walked out to retrieve her, and she flopped on her side and rolled in the grass. Then something spooked her, and she scampered into a bush. I followed her, hoping to get her back in the house. I stepped on a dead palm frond, and it crackled underfoot, spooking her again. She dashed down a path and around the side of the house. I followed, but now she was gone.

I searched the yard and the property, calling her name, for more than thirty minutes and then walked back into the garage. Something compelled me to look up, and there she was, sitting on the rafters just above my car. Relief flooded through me, and I tapped the roof of my car, motioning for her to jump down. She did, and I scooped her into my arms and got her into the house.

Now that I knew she could safely seek refuge in the garage, I let her out to explore the yard for short periods if I was home because I knew it was important for cats to have some outside time. Cats process emotions for us that get trapped in their bodies. In order to release what they've processed, they need to connect with the earth. When they are able to paw and scratch and roll in the dirt, they release and reground. Just as humans need to cleanse to release toxins that build up in our bodies, in order to stay healthy. So while I worried about her being out of my sight when she was outside, I knew it was important for her well-being. When she went out, I would visualize her in a protective bubble to keep her safe, and after thirty minutes I would call her name and shake a bag of treats. She never wandered far and would always come when called. She was almost dog-like in that respect.

Our routine was simple. Mornings, she lounged by my feet while I answered emails. Mid-morning was playtime, and she'd chase a tail she'd ripped off a toy mouse that I'd tied to a string, leaping and flipping like a feline acrobat. Afternoons were all about napping, and evenings she slept at the foot of the bed.

She loved anything that smelled like horses because it reminded her of her first home. I had a shoulder guard lying on the floor that I'd brought home from the ranch to wash. Made of stretchable nylon, it belonged to my horse, Bear, and he would wear it in the summer and fall to protect him from rubbing his chest raw. She would pounce on it and roll around on it, inhaling the smell that reminded her of the ranch. It was the cutest thing.

Willow was an adorable girl and very conversational. When I spoke to her, she'd gurgle a polite response from deep in her throat. On the first evening she was with me, I was preparing for bed. I walked down the hall, and when I turned to look back, she was at the far end of the hall watching me. I think she assumed I was going to go to bed without her. When I called her, she gurgled, leapt straight in the air, and dashed down the hall. Her behavior was so reminiscent of my last cat, Kanga, that it was like having her back with me. So many of Willow's behaviors reminded me of Kanga. Her gurgling, the way she followed me like a dog. The way she came when I called even when she was outside. It was such a gift having her with me.

One morning, I let her into the closed garage to snoop and poke into the dark recesses looking for mice. About thirty minutes later, she jumped up on the ledge of the door that led from the garage to the family room, hanging by her front paws and peering through the window into the room. I was sitting just feet away at my computer, and my heart lurched. The only cat I'd ever had who had done that had been Kanga.

I began to wonder if Willow was Kanga, returned to me in a different form. But when I tuned into my intuition for answers, I heard only silence. I emailed Jill and asked her. Her response was that she wasn't being told anything either, so it probably wasn't Kanga. But it didn't matter. It was like having her back again, and I savored every minute of it.

Willow gave me my second scare two months into her stay with me. On Christmas day, my family and I came home to find that she hadn't eaten the dinner I'd left her. I thought it was odd, but my experience with my other cats had taught me that cats sometimes don't eat. The next morning, she refused to eat again, so I texted her family to see if she had ever done this with them. The mom responded that it was probably the change in the weather. It had been extremely warm for days, and then a cold snap had set in.

But an online search revealed that refusal to eat for twenty-four hours was serious, so that afternoon, I took her to the vet. They found nothing. She was a little dehydrated, but that was it. They gave her a dose of antacid and a shot of anti-nausea medication, hydrated her under the skin with a syringe, and sent me home with more antacids to administer over the next few days.

She continued to go downhill. I tuned into her using my intuition, and she said her tummy was off but that she would be OK. I felt there was more to it, so I reached out to two people, Jill and my friend Jayme, a holistic energy healer, who promised to come the next day.

Jill responded via email the next morning. She said Willow was heartbroken. And she missed her family. It made sense, but the timing was confusing. She hadn't been with her family in over two months. Was this something new, or had she always felt this way? I hadn't picked up on any sadness prior to this. When Jayme arrived, Willow was curled up on an electric blanket I'd plugged in for her.

Jayme approached her slowly and dug a white stone and a blue crystal from her pouch and set them in front of her. Willow gingerly sniffed the white stone but retreated from the other, and Jayme removed it. Then she held her hands over Willow's back and tummy.

"She's sad. Do you know why?" she asked.

"She misses her family. When she first came to me, my guides told me that she had an important purpose with the family. The dad was in a bad accident that severely injured his foot. He's had eleven operations to repair it, and none have been successful. He finally made the decision to amputate his leg at the knee and get a prosthetic. I was told that Willow was instrumental in his healing process. I sort of scoffed when they told me this because the dad has had such a horrible time. But their response was that, without Willow, he might not have lived."

"Why isn't she with them?"

"Their new ranch is in upheaval. Heavy equipment coming in and out every day. There's no fence, and their property backs up to a preserve, so they're worried the cats would get out and get lost. Their dogs are there, but they keep wandering off too, so it's just chaos. They want to get everything settled before they move the cats."

"Well, she doesn't understand why she isn't with them," Jayme said, continuing to draw energy from Willow. "What confuses me is her behavior. I'm sensing she's been sad for a while. Why would she stop eating now?"

"I don't know," I replied. "It's baffling to me."

Within ten minutes, Willow got up and strolled away.

"She's done," Jayme said.

That evening, Willow perked up. She played. Dashed up and down the hall after me and even ate some treats. I was hopeful that she was on the mend. But the next morning, I could tell she was shutting down again. She refused anything I offered. I tried tuna, poached chicken, chicken broth, salmon, sardines, and her favorite treats. She wouldn't even approach food and seemed repulsed by anything I offered. I contacted the family, and the mom texted me to meet her at the vet the next day. She had an 8:00 a.m. appointment to get her new kitten spayed.

Her answer floored me. They had a new kitten? I tried to stay out of judgment. I didn't know the whole story, but I was deeply confused by their actions. And now Willow's situation made sense. Our animal companions pick up on every nuance of our lives. So often, I've told my horse about something that is happening to me, and his response is always, "I know." Willow knew about the kitten. She knew she'd been replaced. And now she'd lost all hope of being reunited with her family. She'd lost her sense of purpose and her role as energetic caregiver to the husband. And now, she was losing her will to live.

I met the mom at the vet and parked my car next to hers. As I took Willow's carrier out of the car, I shivered from nerves and the bracing winter air. Willow's mom nestled her new kitten in the pouch of her coat and carried her indoors.

While we waited for the vet, I took Willow from her carrier and told the mom everything I had learned about Willow in the time she'd been with me. I told her that I knew it all sounded crazy, but I trusted my intuition. Willow butted her head into me over and over, rubbing on my sweatshirt and purring for the first time in days. I could feel her joy at seeing her mom. She was euphoric. I could hear her saying, *Thank you, thank you, thank you. You're making my dream come true. I'm going home.*

"Dobie," Willow's mom said, "I can't take her to the new ranch. She'll be miserable there. It's like a war zone."

"But she's primarily an indoor cat," I said, protesting. "Can't she just stay in the house? And take walks with you to and from the barn? She'd be so happy. She'll stay by your side. It's what she does with me when I let her out."

"I'm just afraid she'd get out and get lost. As it is, the dogs are always escaping, and our neighbors are beginning to complain."

"But without your family, she's lost her purpose, and she feels replaced. There's nothing physically wrong with her. She's just broken-hearted. I bet she'd even nibble some food right now, she's so happy seeing…" My voice trailed off.

"Maybe the best thing is to take her back to the old ranch," she said. "I'll text the renters and ask them if they'll take care of her."

The vet walked in, halting our conversation. She examined Willow and took blood to run tests. Willow's mom had to leave for work, so I waited for the test results. After twenty minutes, the vet sat with me in the lobby. And confirmed my thoughts. The tests revealed nothing. They sent me home with appetite stimulants and a syringe to hand-feed Willow watered-down canned food.

If I couldn't get her eating within twenty-four hours, she'd have to go on a feeding tube. I left the vet stressed and worried. My heart was pounding in my throat at the knowledge that Willow's life was in my hands now. The vet's words echoed in my ears. She had stared into my eyes and gravely said, "You've got to get this cat to eat."

I left the vet, settled Willow in the car, and checked my phone. I saw that I had a text from Karen, who was renting the ranch where Willow had lived. Karen was offering to keep her. But when I asked about whether Willow could be indoors, she replied that they could try but they had a cat-crazy dog, so it would depend on whether Willow could stand up to him. The more we talked, the more I realized that it wasn't in Willow's best interests to return there. And even though I felt that Karen and her partner might be more successful in getting Willow to eat because they wouldn't stress about it the way I would, I couldn't take her back there.

Willow talked to me the entire drive home, meowing incessantly. She didn't know she wasn't going home to her mom. When I let her out of the carrier and she saw she was back home with me, her euphoria dissipated. I could feel her disappointment and the impending emotional shutdown. I was devastated for her.

I did more research on methods to stimulate appetite and tried them all. Oregano on the food. Bonito flakes. High-calorie, super-flavorful gel. She refused everything. My daughter and I took turns syringing food into her mouth. But the syringe was tricky, and air pockets caused the contents to burst and splatter. I got more food on her than in her, but it was a start.

Later that day, I gave Jayme an update on Willow and my conversation with the mom. Jayme said she had fallen in love with Willow and wanted to take her when she moved to her new ranch in a few months. It made sense. I felt that Willow needed to be in a home where there was more going on. Willow needed to be reunited with all of the elements of her first life that she loved so much. She was raised with dogs and cats and horses, and Jayme could offer her that. And she needed to be with a family that would make her a priority and focus on helping her heal. Jayme was the perfect solution. And although Willow wasn't really mine to give, I felt that being with Jayme might be best for her. Ironically, Willow also reminded Jayme of a cat she had had in the past. She told me that, the first moment she met Willow, she too felt that Willow was the incarnation of her first kitty. So adopting Willow almost seemed fated. But it was still contingent on getting Willow to eat and reconnected with her will to live.

"This whole thing is so stressful for me," I said to Jayme. "My heart is pounding out of control, and all I want to do is cry. To see her so euphoric at the vet when she thought she was there to go home with her mom and then completely shut down later was the saddest thing I've ever witnessed."

"That's because you're an empath," she said. "You're feeling everything she's feeling."

"That's interesting because I've had a slightly acid stomach all day. I wonder if that's her stomach I'm feeling."

"Probably. When it goes away, you'll know she's on the mend." Then she paused and said, "You know, I haven't even considered having a cat since 1990 when I lost my darling girl, Precious. I had rescued her and was devastated when six months later she got out of the house and was hit by a car."

"When Willow came into my life," I said, "I could feel my heart begin to heal in regard to losing Kanga. Maybe she'll do that for you too."

When I returned home, I tuned into Willow, sobbing while I talked to her. I told her that I understood her pain and that everyone at some point experiences a broken heart. I knew what it did to one's desire to eat or function or live. I told her that this situation would pass and that everything happens for a reason. I told her that she was a beautiful, special, amazing being and that I could foresee a future for her that held so much joy. More joy than she could imagine. I told her I'd found her an amazing home, and they were already in love with her. That so many people were ready to love her.

"But you've got to start eating, kitten," I said through my tears. "Don't make me watch you die. Don't ask me to do that. I love you too much. It would destroy me."

That night, she ate a few treats, and the next day even more. But I worried about her water intake. If she got dehydrated, she'd stop eating the little bit that she was now. I syringed water into her mouth. It was a process we were both beginning to hate. And I wondered why she even allowed me to approach her anymore. I was constantly shoving food or water or pills in her mouth. Each time I did, I told her that I was sorry but I had to do it to make her well.

The next day, Jayme returned to work on her again. I told her about my conversation with Willow. She listened and sat next to her on the sofa and cupped her hands inches from Willow's midsection. Willow stretched out, her head and arms hanging off the sofa cushions and then flipped on her back to allow Jayme full access to her torso.

"She's so much better," Jayme said.

"Is she still sad?"

"No," she said, shaking her head.

"How did she release it so quickly?"

"She has closure. And I think your little talk with her had an impact."

After a few minutes, Willow slid off the sofa and lay under the coffee table. A few moments later, she hopped back up on the sofa next to Jayme for another three-minute session.

That night, I put treats and kibble in a dish for her. She'd started eating and drinking a little more but still refused to eat anything but treats, and I was getting desperate to get her back on real food. The next morning, the pile of treats I had put in her food dish was gone and her water dish was almost empty. I hoped she was on the road to recovery, but I was cautiously optimistic, fearing that we were still not out of the woods. Within a few days, she was back to eating normally. And I could finally relax.

Several weeks later, I sent Willow's mom an email telling her I'd met someone who wanted to adopt Willow. I described the lifestyle Willow would have. A human companion who worked from home. A home that she could share with dogs and horses. A home where she could be a priority. A life with an energy worker who would sense any imbalances and address them before they became an issue. Most important, someone who would treat her like family and love her wholeheartedly. I asked her how she felt about Willow going to this new home. She responded within a few days that it was OK, but if anything changed, she wanted Willow to come and live with them.

While she waited to be able to make Willow hers, Jayme came to my house several times a week to visit her and bond. Willow seemed to love the attention and was often almost flirtatious, rolling around near where Jayme lay on the floor, reaching out to her with her paws, peering coyly at her, partially hidden under a blanket.

"I've thought about her a lot since meeting her," Jayme said. "She reminds me so much of Precious that, like I said, I've found myself wondering if she's come back to me through Willow."

"I've wondered that too," I said. "In fact, it occurred to me when you told me you hadn't had a cat since Precious."

Now that Willow was completely healed, I bought her a new toy to celebrate. Several feathers attached to a swivel joint and a line affixed to a stick. When activated, it whistled through the air, mimicking the sound and movement of a bird in flight. Willow was nuts for it. She'd stalk it for hours, leaping and flipping in the air in her attempts to capture it. It was as though I'd unleashed her inner hunter.

And she became more comfortable play-attacking me out of the blue. One moment we'd be sitting peacefully side by side. The next, she'd leap at my arm, biting and clawing me. But she was always quick to back off if I yelped, "Ow!"

When I told Jayme about the new toy and her obsession with it, she raised her eyebrows and said, "You need to prepare her for the fact that she'll be sharing her home with a parrot."

The next day, I tuned into Willow and told her about the parrot.

Don't worry. I know the difference between a family member and real prey.

As I reflected on Willow's story, I wondered about her purpose in my life. I knew Willow was a healer. She'd worked wonders with her first family, healed my broken heart, and now was preparing to enter Jayme's life and heal her wounds in regard to her last kitty. But I wondered: Was I just a pit stop on her journey to a different future? Was I simply destined to be a matchmaker to pair her with someone new? Or had our time together had a more significant purpose? When I tuned into her, I heard the phrase *significant pairing*. I didn't know whether the word *pairing* referred to her and me or the fact that I had brought her and Jayme together.

Then I heard my guides.

You were a catalyst. Willow was attached to the idea that she was going to be reunited with her family. She would have wasted away waiting. And she wouldn't have thrived at the new ranch, but she was fixated on being there with her family. She needed a mental breakthrough to release her from her attachments to that outcome. You allowed her to come to terms with her grief, and now she sees there truly is love on the other side. She believed you when you told her that what she lost would be regained a thousand times once she reconstructs and discovers a new foundation of faith and hope in herself and in life. Often, we cannot see the forest for the trees. Becoming one with her feelings is a crucial step on the path of life. With faith and hope, she was able to heal her broken heart and to love herself. There is no love greater than self-love. There is no power greater than that.

Then I was shown a picture. Of a maiden imprisoned in a tower. It was Rapunzel. Like Rapunzel, Willow too had been locked in a tower of sorts, held in place by her desires and her attachment to an outcome that might have not been in her highest interest anymore. She too waited to be rescued by her family. But in the end, she chose to open her heart, to heal, and to love herself. And in doing so, she rescued herself.

Spec and Eunice

"On the last day of our riding holiday," Eunice said, laughing, "everyone else in our group was buying souvenirs, maple syrup, and trinkets. And I...I bought a horse."

She'd been looking for a horse for some time. A lover of horses since childhood, she'd always wanted one. And her search during adulthood led her to the more unusual breeds.

"I started looking at the curly breeds because I'm allergic. But I was drawn to anything exotic," she said. "Yet for some reason, I never followed through with any of the horses I looked at."

Several years ago, and well into a search for a horse, a friend suggested they take a riding vacation in Vermont, and the idea seemed idyllic. Riding quietly in the lush, rolling countryside through green meadows flanked by deep, thick forests.

The horses they would ride on this holiday were Icelandics, a smallish, pony-like yet hearty breed known for their willing personalities, affinity for humans, and stamina. Considered the world's purest breed, Icelandic horses were brought by Viking ships to serve as the sole source of transportation over Iceland's rough terrain. In addition to the walk, trot, and canter, Icelandic horses also tölt, a four-beat running walk that produces fluid, rhythmic, forward movement and pace, an exhilarating racing gait that can be performed at speeds up to thirty miles per hour. Eventually, the breed made its way to the United States.

On the farm they visited in Vermont, Eunice was paired with a jet-black gelding with a dense mane and forelock that cascaded over his eyes. His name, Speckengeur (Spec for short), meant genius.

"The trip was amazing," she said. "I wasn't the greatest rider back then, but the Icelandics are so smooth, and I loved the tölt and could sit it for long periods of time. I rode several horses on the trip, and I had to work to stay in the saddle before I was paired with Spec. But with Spec, it was effortless. This horse made me feel competent. And I felt an instant connection. As though I had known him before. And by the end of our short trip, and with some deep consideration, I made the decision to purchase him and bring him back to California."

Eunice purchased and coordinated delivery of everything she needed to prepare to bring Spec to her home. She bought tack and grooming supplies, scheduled a vet check, and organized the transport from Vermont to California. And although Spec was the farm owner's personal horse, she agreed to let him go. Shipping him to California by truck and trailer would take almost a week.

"When the hauler unloaded him from the trailer, I could tell he was disoriented and depressed. I don't know how many stops they made, but the interior of the trailer was dark, and his eyes didn't adjust to the light once they unloaded him. He ran around our fields and crashed into a tree. I was horrified. It was in that moment that I saw things from his point of view. He'd lost the person he was most connected to, his home, his herd. Everything. And everything here was new. And I vowed to provide him with the best home that I could."

And so they began their journey together. At first, Spec was the supreme gentleman. Standing quietly while Eunice mounted him. Chilling when tied for grooming. Quiet on the trails. But then, sensing her lack of experience with riding and horses, he began to test her. He'd take off under saddle, fidget while she attempted to mount, and push the pace faster than she was comfortable with.

One day, he escaped from his stall and got into a bag of alfalfa and molasses, a sweet feed meant to increase energy and calorie intake. In large quantities, it can induce the equivalent of a sugar high. Later that day, he promptly bucked Eunice off when she saddled him and mounted, unaware of his sweets-induced energy.

After that, she sought the advice of a trainer. They started from scratch, beginning first with ground work. Then they progressed to lunging on a lunge line, where Eunice would ride without stirrups or reins, establishing balance and communication through her seat.

"We were a long way from perfect as a riding duo, but otherwise it was as though we had been together forever," Eunice said. "It was like we were interconnected and interdependent. Like we spoke a language no one else knew. He gave me a challenge as a rider, but on the other hand, I was the only person who could catch him."

After a few months, Eunice felt confident enough to work with Spec on her own but contacted a psychic to learn more about the inner workings of her new horse. The psychic told Eunice that she needed to sit her saddle, that when she rode she wasn't completely connected to her horse. Then she told her that Spec was an ambassador and that Eunice wasn't treating him properly. The reading left her more confused than illuminated. Spec had begun acting up on the trails, taking off and bolting. Eunice reached out to me to come and meet Spec and to learn what I could about him.

When I arrived at her ranch, it was late afternoon. Spec shared the ranch with several other horses, and they all munched their dinnertime hay contentedly. I approached Spec, and he raised his head to look at me. Not wanting to disturb him, I sat quietly on one of the rungs of his pipe corral. Then I tuned into him while he ate. Eunice slid next to me and sat on the same pipe bar, and as I spoke to Spec, I relayed what I was hearing to Eunice.

"What's going on out on the trail?" I asked. "What is happening to you out there?"

No response from him, but I heard my guides' voices. They told me that what he was experiencing wasn't fear or panic; he was overwhelmed by the chaos, the other riders and horses around him.

I took the information and ran it past him. "So I understand that it's not fear that you're running from but the need to escape the chaos of the others. Do you know that you can protect yourself energetically? It's like setting up an invisible shield. Do you know how to do that?"

Sort of. But it seems like a lot of trouble.

I shrugged. "Well, it's either that or continue to terrorize Eunice with your bolting. Could you trust Eunice to do this for the both of you?"

I don't know that I trust her to have that skill.

Suddenly, I realized what he was telling me. He lacked confidence in Eunice's riding ability, and that influenced his confidence in everything else. He loved her, but he didn't respect her.

"Spec, you need to be willing to acknowledge that just because Eunice doesn't have years of riding experience doesn't mean she isn't advanced enough to protect you spiritually and energetically."

His head shot up, and he eyed me suspiciously, chewing his hay in a slightly circular motion. He was mulling this over. Literally chewing on the information I had offered. I knew I had gotten through to him. Then I heard my guides.

He has a royalty complex. Many horses do. They consider themselves above it all. Especially above humans, since most haven't learned to speak their language. With Spec, he demands that those who ride him prove themselves worthy.

I tuned into Spec again. "So I understand that you consider yourself to be like a king. Here's something to consider then when you are out on the trail. When a king's castle is under siege, or in the midst of chaos, the king must stand his ground. Strong, unfazed, and unwavering in his courage. He cannot allow the chaos to affect him or it affects his people. The king must be the role model for others."

No response from him. More staring and chewing.

"What do you need from Eunice?" I asked.

Discipline. Not in the way most humans think of it. Not harsh. I need consistency. The way you'd raise a child. I need clear boundaries. I need to know where she stands. And while I don't enjoy it, I can see the merits of groundwork.

"What do you…" I began.

I'm done. Then he went back to eating.

"He's done," I said to Eunice. "One other thing I am being told. When you ride him, visualize a pole going through your center, through him, and touching the ground. It will help you stay with him when he bolts or gets crazy."

"Would you like to ride him?"

"No, he's eating," I said. "And I want our conversation to sink in."

But Eunice insisted, leading him from his stall and saddling him. I had brought three girlfriends with me, and I laughed and told everyone not to expect too much since it would be my first time on him and I'd never ridden a gaited horse.

Eunice coached me on the signals to queue the tölt once he was warmed up. She told me to close my legs on him and lean back slightly, letting my seat go with his motion. Spec executed every queue perfectly. It was as though I'd ridden him for years. Even my friends commented that, although they knew nothing about riding, they could tell I was an accomplished rider. But I knew our successful ride had more to do with Spec's cooperation than with my skill. Then I heard my guides.

You listened to him. So he listened to you.

To increase her awareness of Spec emotionally, Eunice began to work with me to develop her skills as an animal communicator. She was a fast and natural learner and even in our first sessions was able to tune in and gain the same messages as I.

She continued to work on her skills and attended a one-day equine clinic where she could work one on one with a talented trainer from the East Coast. The trainer diagnosed Spec as a very tense horse who needed to let off steam through exercise. Eunice learned to make some minor adjustments to her tack that would make Spec more comfortable. Then the trainer told her that her nerves compounded Spec's tension. During the clinic, Spec and another horse shared a shallow platform. Spec wanted to be front and center. With almost undetectable sidesteps, he slowly moved the other horse off the platform until he stood alone.

"It amused me," Eunice said, "and it showed me how clever he was and that I'd need to keep his mind busy to ease his tension."

One day, Eunice saddled Spec to ride, put her foot in the stirrup and was just ready to swing into the saddle. A horse tied next to them in the barn spooked, and Spec shot down the barn stall like a rocket, dragging Eunice behind him. She broke her back in three places.

"After that, Spec wouldn't look at me, and he moped for days. He felt so bad, and I wondered if my only option was to give him up. Clearly, he was too much horse for me. But the thought made me so sad. And him too. We were both just so sad. I tried one more thing. I got him a playmate."

Eunice brought another Icelandic to meet Spec. But they didn't click. So Eunice brought another one. A caramel-colored mare named Fidla with a bushy blonde mane and tail. She was adorable. Calm. Sweet. Uncomplicated. Spec and Fidla bonded immediately.

Next, Eunice turned to her friend Wendy, who was an experienced equestrian, to work with her and Fidla, hoping the mellow mare would help her build both her skills and her confidence. The trainer worked with Eunice to hone the skill of the involuntary dismount to gain the ability to bail from the horse if things got too intense.

"Wendy taught me to look for a safe place to jump off, to bail if things felt unsafe. So that's what I practiced on Fidla. Over and over. It was so easy on Fid. She was so stoic in comparison to Spec's nerves. But she was stubborn. Contrary to Spec's need for movement, Fidla didn't want to budge. I had to work on getting her more forward-moving, while, with Spec, I was always holding him back and in constant fear. Fidla gave me the confidence to get back up on Spec."

Once Eunice regained her confidence, Wendy had her start working with Spec again. And they went back to the basics. Starting with groundwork. The basis for creating a common language.

"Wendy showed me so much. Much of it was being able to read and work with energy. And to use my body to influence his. We started in the round pen, working on a lunge line. I learned to influence his course of direction through the placement of my body. If I was slightly behind him, it was a driving cue, signaling him to continue moving forward. If I stepped slightly in front of him, it was a cue for him to halt. If I continued approaching, it was a signal not only to stop but to change direction. It was like a dance, and once I understood the choreography, we didn't step on each other's toes anymore," she said and then laughed.

"When I became more refined in the work, I could send him forward simply by pushing energy toward him. Then I'd visualize withdrawing the energy to encourage him to come toward me. I didn't realize I'd use this later to break up fights when we added a third herd member."

Once they had refined the subtleties of energy exchange, Wendy had the pair go back to basic training under saddle. Backing, sidepassing, and moving off the leg. She taught Eunice to be the leader.

"He already knows you love him," Wendy told her. "But you've got to be the leader. Don't negotiate. Give him clear cues and allow him to respond. If you get nervous, you'll trigger it in him."

Several years later, Eunice added a third Icelandic to the herd, intended to be her partner's horse. A stunning caramel-blonde mare with black socks and a luxuriously thick black mane and tail shocked with blond shards. Her name was Bjork.

Not long after Bjork joined the family, Eunice hosted a party to introduce her to family and friends. When I arrived, she walked me down to the horses. Each stood in a separate stall. Spec separated the two mares. I greeted Spec and Fidla and turned my attention to Bjork.

"Tell me about yourself," I said.

I'm special.

She refused to interact with me beyond that.

Eunice and her partner had set up drinks and appetizers in the bed of a trailer hooked to a quad. Since the entire area was fenced, I suggested to Eunice that we let the horses out to join the party. They trotted around, and everyone laughed when Spec tried to gain access to the tortilla chips. I stood at the hood of the quad, watching the mares interact. Suddenly, they were butt to butt, kicking each other violently and screaming. I jumped back a few feet, worried they might come my way. And Eunice screamed at the mares to stop. Spec turned on his heels and sped toward them, separating the fight. And Eunice and her partner quickly returned the horses to their enclosures.

"I should have anticipated that. I'm sorry," I told Eunice later. "I knew they didn't get along, but I thought the presence of people and a celebration would divert their focus from each other."

The next day, I had an email from Eunice asking me

to tune into Bjork and ask what she meant when she said she was special. Then Eunice went on to tell me that that morning Spec and Fidla had been in their stall and Bjork and pushed her way through the gate to get at them. Bjork and Fidla had gone at it again, and Spec had tried his best to break things up.

Hearing the commotion, she'd run toward the barn screaming, and the fighting stopped. Both Spec and Bjork were cut. Eunice bent over, head in her hands, and started to cry.

I don't know what to do, her email continued. *Spec and Fidla came over to stand with me and nuzzle my hair. They would not leave my side. I held Spec in my arms and cried. Then I spoke with Spec and said I really needed his help. He said he was doing his best. I spoke with Fid and told her she had to be above this and that it was making me very sad and scared someone would get hurt. She said she just did not like Bjork. I could not get through to Bjork at all. We stood there a long time. Bjork tried a few more times to shove her head through and bite Fidla. All is quiet now. I think Bjork was brought up alone and does not know how to be in a herd. Maybe leaving them all out with no place to go so that they can work through it is the only solution. But that worries me. I don't want anyone to get hurt. Can you please tune into Bjork and talk to her?*

I did as she asked and emailed a response:

I know. It's so violent. Even the little bit I saw yesterday at the party unnerved me as well because it's not playful at all. The horses in my horse's pastures will play with each other, but it's never that violent. I can understand how devas-

tating this is.

Yesterday may have been a catalyst for what happened today because so many people were there and they were allowed to be part of the complete herd, which set off a new level of competition. Again, I'm sorry I didn't see that coming.

Bjork is a diva, and I say that without judgment. So she expects everyone to treat her like royalty. Part of this is because she knows her look is unique, and she's been fawned over so it fuels that in her. I went into her energy and tried to connect and get her to understand that her behavior isn't acceptable. Her response was that she doesn't care what I think. I couldn't really connect with her at all. She doesn't want any part of that. I told her that, if she couldn't get along, she might have to leave, and she doesn't care about that either. I'm getting that she isn't able to bond easily. She thinks she was born to be in charge.

I reached out to a friend who is an energy worker, but she doesn't believe there is much she could do. This is a behavioral, territorial issue between two emotional females. One who believes she should be in charge because she is en-titled and one who believes she should be in charge because she was there first.

Maybe it would help to sage the barn and area to clear the energy. You'll have to do this at least once a week, but it could keep the animosity from building up between them. If you let them all together to sort out the herd pecking order, it will probably work…but not without injury.

Eunice followed my advice and things calmed down a

little. But the mares still have their issues from time to time and always will. Spec is housed between them. A buffer of sorts, keeping the peace. But no matter what, all three will be with Eunice for life. In the years since Spec has been with her, he and Eunice have formed a deep bond.

"How would you describe your connection and how it's changed over the years?"

"I know his thoughts," she said. "He's taught me to deal with his energy. And with the help of a gifted trainer, now I ride him like an Icelandic. I've learned a lot about connecting and protecting us energetically. I visualize a blue triangle surrounding us from my waist to the ground and around that visualize white light. And I've learned to trust my own advancement as a rider. Now I allow him to move out like he was intended to move. I talk to him, and I treat him like an equal."

When I asked her to describe his personality, she reverted to her roots as a doctor of psychology. "He's a high C," she said, describing one of the personality types in the Myers Brigg temperament assessment.

A high C is meticulous, careful, and precise. Which describes Spec's style of descending steep slopes on the trail. One hoof perfectly placed in front of another perfectly placed and another, picking his way down the hill. High Cs are also introverted and brilliant.

"He's super smart," she said with a chuckle. "He can pick locks, open gates, close gates. He's not overly social except with me and Fidla. But on the trail, he likes to lead, and if he's not in front, he's vocal about his disapproval.

He's never aggressive, but he'll find a way to use subtlety to get what he wants."

I asked her why she thought she and Spec came together, and she responded that she thought they had had other lives together and that they had come together to complete something.

"He gives me peace," she said. "It's been a cycle, that's for sure. Fun, fear, work, peace. And now we are old friends. He helps me process life's traumas. And I think he helped me regain my courage."

"What has he taught you?" I asked.

Tears sprang to her eyes, and she didn't answer immediately. When she did speak, her voice was husky from emotion. "So many things. To not give up on someone if you love them. That you can love another species as much as a human. That if you love someone, bad things can happen but that doesn't have to define the future. He taught me that I needed to be a leader. To ride correctly. To balance leadership and partnership. To behave in ways that don't confuse him. To learn his language. That in a true partnership it's not about control; it's about setting up a communication system where leadership is shared."

I asked Spec what his partnership with Eunice had meant to him.

She's a donor.

"I don't understand that."

She's always giving something. There's an energy

exchange. She seems to know what I need, and she loans me the energy to do what's important to me. She doesn't even realize the energy exchange that happens between us. She assumes I am always the one helping her. I am her knight in shining armor, but she is the keeper of my heart.

When we were done communicating, I pulled a deck of cards from my meditation cabinet. The Inner Child Cards developed by Isha Lerner. And I asked for a message to describe the connection between Eunice and Spec. The card I drew was a butterfly being unveiled by two fairies. It represents a magnificent potential of the soul. In Welsh mythology, fairies were known as "the mothers" or "the helpers." These fairies are liberating the spiritual quality of humanity. There is a connection between the soul and the butterfly in Greek mythology. This stems from the belief that the human soul becomes a butterfly while searching for a new incarnation. The process of transformation is extremely powerful in our lives as we search for a broad understanding of the future and a gentle surrender to the past.

Bakari and Dobie

A male lion and his mate perched warily on a stretch of sand on a rocky cliff overlooking the ocean. A breeze ruffled the male's mane slightly. I thought it odd that these wild lions would be here, so far from their natural habitat. Although I hadn't witnessed it, I knew the pair had been harassed by the group of departing men making their way down the cliff. And now, with their trust in humans compromised, they had turned their eyes toward me and my six-year-old son. I instantly assumed we were in danger and hastily telepathed as calmly as I could, I mean you no harm, but if you injure my son, there will be consequences. *The male rose and approached me, his immense paws splayed out with each purposeful step. When he was near enough, he softly butted my thigh with his head. And I knelt, inhaling the pungent odor from his mane and feeling the heat of his breath on my face. Then he leaned into me, rubbing my chest with his immense jaw, like a domestic feline would. I wove his luxurious fur in my fingers and cradled his head in my arms, savoring the connection with this noble creature.*

Two years ago, this had been only a dream. Little did I know that a real lion was about to have a profound impact on my life.

Our eyes met and locked. For a five-second span, his gaze penetrated mine. Every cell in my being froze and then clicked back to life, like the second hand on a clock moving from one marker to the next. There was a change in my being that I didn't understand. And it would take me on one of the strangest journeys of my life.

Then he looked away, releasing his hold on me, and settled aloofly with his side to me as he lay on the cropped grass in his enclosure. Bakari was the only male lion we'd meet at the Lions, Tigers, & Bears sanctuary I was visiting with my friend Jill, and his body language was clear. He had already graced me with more attention than he'd intended to.

Powerful and proud, his mane was densely plumed with streaks of bronze, russet, black. Testosterone-fueled muscle and sinew rippled beneath his taut, tan hide. The sanctuary owner had told us that they had kept him intact to preserve his mane.

"Look at how he's tracking the owner," Jill said as the woman made her way back up the hill to the offices. "He's fixated on her. He knows that she was the one who saved him."

It was true. As soon as Bakari saw her leave, he rose and galloped along the side of his enclosure until he reached the wall. I found myself wondering what it would be like to have such a wild creature so deeply connected to you.

Jill and I continued strolling through the sanctuary. It was fall, and a warm Santa Ana wind blew in off the desert and swirled around us, mingling with the cooler coastal breeze that tempered the heat of the sun.

An outgoing, plump, pale-orange and white tabby cat followed us as we walked, flopping on his back to invite a tummy rub when we slowed our pace or stopped. I joked to one of the volunteers that I was surprised he wasn't skittish around all the wild energy from the big cats. She laughed and explained that Tom had joined the sanctuary as a feral kitten eleven years ago and was the resident greeter. "He thinks everyone is here to see him," she said.

Bakari, we learned, had come to the Lions, Tigers & Bears sanctuary with his two sisters, Suri and Jillian, at the age of four weeks. Rescued from a sanctuary in Louisiana. Due to overcrowding in their facility, they were unable to keep the cubs. Lions, Tigers & Bears stepped in and accepted all three lion cubs.

As the "boy" of the litter, Bakari was a bit laid back and let his sisters fend for him but wasn't afraid to show them who was boss. His name was an African expression that translated meant "one with great promise."

We walked back toward the tigers we'd met earlier. A large man stood in front of one of the female tigers' enclosure. We came closer to observe her, and she sprang toward the fence, snaring it with all four paws, snarling viciously at the man as she clung to the chain link. Her guttural growl vibrated through my core. I jumped, gripping Jill's arm, my fingers digging into her skin. Two walls of chain link fencing separated us. But the violent attack drove her point home. We were among giants who could crush us with a single swipe of a paw. The keeper told us that, when the tigress had been in utero, her mother had been mistreated by a man and that, although she'd never witnessed the event, she was still skittish in the presence of male energy.

"Cellular memory," Jill whispered. "She could sense what was happening to her mother." We left the female and then slowed in front of a playful, happy-go-lucky male tiger batting a ball tethered to the ceiling of his enclosure. Maverick had been confiscated by California Department of Fish and Wildlife from a celebrity who did not have the proper license to own an exotic animal. He came to the sanctuary in 2014 when he was about nine months old. His birthday was two days after mine.

"Ask him if he's happy," Jill said. I was surprised she'd asked me to do it. She's far more sentient than I am. Information comes to her easily, while I still have to focus, concentrate, and work for the messages I get.

I tuned into Maverick, and I heard nothing. "He's not communicating," I said. I tried again. Nothing. The cat was either blocking me or was uninterested in communicating. Then I tuned into my guides.

He's happy. More accurate...he's at peace. He realizes that his life here is much better than it would have been elsewhere, and it's more natural. He understands that his caretakers love him and take their job seriously. Maverick's not trying to block you. The wild ones aren't used to having humans try to communicate. It's foreign to them, and they don't generally seek out human contact the way a domestic cat or dog would. You and he needed a translator to communicate. That's where we come in.

I shared the message with Jill, who nodded.

We explored other exhibits at the sanctuary, meeting goats, burros, and chickens before leaving for lunch. But the encounter with Bakari lingered like a haunting memory I couldn't shake.

That night, my lifelong battle with insomnia ratcheted to a new level. It would be a year before I would understand the effect his gaze had had on my body.

That night, when the sun set, I found myself tiring to the point of exhaustion even though it was early. I could feel almost an obsession with falling asleep creep into my mind and body. But as tired as I was, I could feel every cell in my body vibrating. It was almost like I was waging a war with a mind that wanted to sleep and a body that was unable to.

The next time I saw Jill, I told her that, since our visit to the sanctuary, I had become almost obsessed with falling asleep when the sun set. She said it was simply my body's desire to attune to the rhythms of the nature kingdom. This made partial sense. Many of the animals I'd met that day did in fact wind down when the sun set. But the opposite was true of the big cats who often hunt at night.

Three months later, I was in Sacramento visiting a friend. We made appointments to see a psychic she often goes to. This was my fourth reading with Paula.

I lay flat on her table, inhaling and exhaling deeply as instructed. I was almost in a meditative state when I heard myself ask a question. One simple question.

"Paula, why don't I sleep?"

"I'm being told that it's past-life related," she said, sweeping a large feather through the air over my body. "I'll see what comes up in our session."

The music swelled slightly. Drums beat and chimes tinkled. My body relaxed, and I floated. As I drifted off, visions began to manifest.

I am a man. Standing on a mountain top, surveying a deep, rugged valley. My arms outstretched, I rotate, hovering slightly above the ground. I have been persecuted. Then I am transported elsewhere. A massive tiger is attacking someone. I am transported again. A brown bear is chasing a young boy. I am transported again. A huge, shimmering egg looms before me, pulsating white, glowing light made of thousands of crystal triangles. I walk toward it and through its sparkling walls. When I am in the center, the walls collapse and form the shape of a lotus, and a beam of light pulls me upward toward Heaven.

Paula's voice pulled me back to earth. "We're done," she said softly. Slowly, I opened my eyes and sat up. I shared with her what I had seen in meditation, and she began to tell me about the lifetimes she saw. The first vision I had on the mountain top represented a lifetime when I had been a cavalry officer. I had fallen asleep on my watch, high on a hill that overlooked our camp. Our camp was overrun by Indians. Many men lost their lives. And the women and children were kidnapped. I was executed for failing to protect the people I was watching over. In another, I was a young boy being chased by a large bear. I was alone in the forest without protection, and the bear mauled me horribly and then lumbered off. In another, I was a sailor on a ship. I had fallen asleep in the crow's nest, and pirates had overtaken the ship and killed many on board before executing me. The next lifetime she detailed mirrored another vision I had seen while she worked on me. I lived in Africa, and I was a safari guide. A young man of around nineteen years old, I was supposed to be watching over the camp. Instead, I fell asleep and was attacked by a big cat and killed. She said she had been shown a lion, not a tiger. Then she shared that there had been four to five other lifetimes when I had been a guard and had been forced to stay awake and as a result had been sleep-deprived, which in this lifetime makes me crave the very thing that eludes me. Sleep.

"You equate sleep with death and dying," she said. "When you fell asleep, bad things happened to you and the people you loved. In this lifetime, in order to do your job and do it well, you believe that you must not sleep. Doing your job well is, and was, the most important thing to you. You took great pride in your work, just as you do in this lifetime. There's also a theme about protection. In each of those lives, you were either supposed to be protecting others or you yourself weren't protected. If you don't feel safe, you can't sleep. When did your sleep issues start?"

"I've never slept well," I said. "It began when my children were babies. Waking up at all hours of the night. I never really learned how to get back to sleep. Then I started worrying about how I would afford to send them to college. But everything intensified last fall when my friend Jill and I went to the Lions, Tigers & Bears sanctuary. That's when I began to obsess about falling asleep."

She handed me a deck of cards and asked me to select three. I pulled a lion, a tiger, and a bear. Our eyes met, and I cocked my head to one side and smiled. There are no accidents. As I prepared to leave, she suggested I work with a past-life therapist. "It's one thing to identify the lives that are causing issues, but it's another to resolve the emotional and spiritual karma," she said.

But her reading explained a lot. It explained why I could easily nap in the afternoon or fall back asleep in the wee hours of the morning if I woke. It explained why I had to take something to fall asleep at night. If I didn't, my body would startle and jerk awake as soon as I began to drift off.

That night, I expected I would fall asleep easily since Paula and I had identified the cause of my insomnia. I followed my typical nighttime ritual: two tablets of melatonin and two shots of tequila sipped slowly while I read and waited for drowsiness to finger its way into my brain. I turned the lights off and tried to doze. Instead, every cell in my body vibrated, almost buzzing, like I was on a caffeine-fueled high. After twenty minutes, I knew I wasn't going to fall asleep, and I realized that identifying the cause of my insomnia was only the beginning. The cellular memory of the past was no longer dormant. It was actively coursing through my system. Demanding to be felt, acknowledged, and resolved.

I shared my experience with Jill. And we talked about different paths of resolution. Like Paula, Jill felt that past-life regression and hypnosis might help. I did some research and found a young woman named Trisha about an hour south of me who worked with those modalities. We talked on the phone about her approach, and I went to meet with her.

"Close your eyes and focus on your breathing," Trisha said. "Visualize yourself descending a staircase." Then her voice began to guide me on a journey.

I am about twenty-five years old and dressed in a modest, brown and beige gown made of filmy fabric. I am walking down a spiral staircase into a dungeon. At the bottom of the staircase, a black dragon slumbers. As soon as my foot leaves the last stair and touches the floor, his left eye springs open, yellow and menacing. I approach him slowly and lay a hand on his head. He lowers his head and sleeps again. Why can't I do that? I wondered. Someone whispers, "The dragon is your insomnia." I walk to a wall that offers three choices. A closed glass window, a closed wooden door, and an open archway. I ask my guides which route I should follow, even though I am drawn to the archway. Their response is to choose the archway, the only open passageway. Once through the arch, I am surrounded by jewel-toned flowers, lush trees with limbs that sweep the ground, and butterflies flitting through the air.

One by one, the people connected to lifetimes needing to be cleared present themselves. An army captain trudges in dragging a rifle. I ask him why he clings to his guilt and grief, and then I hug him and tell him he is forgiven. He drops to his knees sobbing, and I place a hand to his head just as I had done with the dragon. I kneel and take him in my arms. Trisha instructs me to send him to the light. I take his hands and bring him to his feet and walk him to the light. He steps into the light, and it consumes him. I turn and collapse, lying on the garden floor until my guides come and pick me up. The next person to come in is the safari guide.

He is dressed in a loincloth. He reminds me of an older version of Mowgli, the jungle boy who is raised by a panther and a bear as they try to protect him from being stalked and killed by Shere Khan, the tiger. He stands in front of me, and Trisha instructs me to tell him he is forgiven and loved. I ask him why he grieves still. He evades my questions. All he will tell me is that his reputation is ruined. I tune into my own intuition and uncover the rest of his story. He wanted to follow in his father's footsteps and become a revered guide. He wanted to make his father proud. Instead, he fell asleep and was killed by a big cat. He felt he had ruined his family's reputation and disgraced them. As I went more deeply into his story, I realized that, in falling asleep and being killed by the cat, he had actually sacrificed himself for the good of the group he was guiding. Had the cat not taken him, it would have killed or maimed others in the safari group. Instead, satiated with his meal of the guide, the cat harmed no one else. In sacrificing himself for the greater good, he'd become a hero. And yet he had no idea. Trisha instructed me to bring his father in.

I visualize the father. He walks directly to his son and takes him in his arms. Tears stream down my face as I witness the reunion. I tell the boy he was a hero, not a coward. The father is crying as he tells his son that his world was shattered when he lost him and that he is so proud of him. They stand embracing, and then I walk them to the light. When they are ready, I release them. Two more lifetimes come in. The sailor and the plantation owner. Both with their particular burden and struggle to release. Both needing love and forgiveness. Both needing to love and forgive themselves. As the plantation owner stood in front of me, crying, his head in his hands, his family floated down from the heavens, and when they touched down, they embraced in a circle, arms intertwined. Then they ascended, soaring upward, until I could no longer see them. Through my tears, I stretched my arms upward and twirled my hands as though to stir the stars.

"When you are ready, open your eyes," Trisha said. I sat in silence for a while, crying quietly, and she handed me a tissue. "Good work."

I visited Trisha several more times to clear other lifetimes that had come up. And worked with Jill to identify more specifics about the lifetimes. Together, we discovered a lifetime where I guarded a pharaoh's tomb. Being impoverished, I stole a jewel but lived in fear that the pharaoh would stalk me from the spirit world. The lifetime in which I was a child running for my life from an attacking bear came up again. As did a life when, as a seven-year-old, I was molested repeatedly by my father at night, and even pretending to be asleep had offered no protection from the repeated attacks. And another life when I had been a warden guarding the inmates, who escaped when I fell asleep. And yet another when I was an army captain, the sole person on watch while everyone else slept.

"The core theme in all these lifetimes is protection or the lack thereof," Jill said. "And now you feel that you have to be an exemplary person to atone for those lifetimes."

Jill felt there were also two sub-themes at work that created a polarity. The first was that, in these past lifetimes, I fell asleep and didn't do my job. Yet, in this lifetime, lack of sleep created anxiety around not functioning to my full capacity in my current job.

"If you don't sleep," she explained, "you can't function. Doing your job well is of utmost importance to you. Which creates anxiety about not being able to get to sleep. The second sub-theme is in regard to being a child. The child who doesn't want to go to sleep for fear of missing out. And diametrically opposed to that is the notion that if you don't go to sleep, Santa Claus won't come. The rewards won't be there. So you've got all these opposing forces at work to resolve. I'm getting that the work you're doing with Trisha and me is important. It resolves the spiritual karma and the subconscious mental and emotional state, but that it isn't going to clear the residue from your body."

She went on to tell me that she had recently met an energy worker named Mary, who used a different form of healing called BodyTalk, and she gave me the contact information.

In my first conversation with Mary, she explained the system in more detail. Mary said that health and body imbalance issues arise for a variety of reasons and that BodyTalk looks at the whole person and their emotional, physical, and environmental influences so that the true underlying causes of dis-ease can be revealed.

"Every choice and every experience in your life has contributed to your current state of health. Each scar, laugh line, and injury has a unique story and a history. Every cell, system, and atom in your body is in constant communication. If any of those connections is disrupted, your body can't communicate and rebalance effectively," she said. "BodyTalk takes each perspective into consideration to establish a personalized approach to rebalancing that brings about lasting changes."

On my first visit to see her, I lay on my back on a thin mattress. Her finger raced back and forth on my forearm like a Geiger counter recording an earthquake.

"I'm establishing what's a 'yes' and 'no' answer from your body," she said and then continued to ask questions to quantify a connection with my body.

"How do you fall asleep now?" she asked.

"I take melatonin, and I sip a couple of shots of tequila before bed," I said. "A nutritionist once used kinesiology to muscle test me for my tolerance for alcohol. Tequila was the best choice for me."

"Because it's plant-based. Not grain- or sugar-based," she said.

"Yeah," I said. "I can't do wine. The sugar either prevents me from dozing off or wakes me up around two in the morning." She continued to ask questions. We identified that the lifetime that was still interfering with my sleep was the safari guide.

"How old were you?" she asked.

"Nineteen," I said.

"I was told before you came in today that there was a lifetime when you were eviscerated," she said.

"I don't know what that means."

"Disemboweled."

"I was attacked by a big cat in that lifetime," I said. "And killed. That's probably where it attacked me."

"What was happening with you in this lifetime at the age of nineteen?"

I told her the first thing that came to my mind. My first significant romantic relationship was ending. Badly.

"How did that make you feel?" she asked.

The word "gutted" flashed through my mind. And I shared it with her.

She nodded and then continued to ask questions until my body had given her the formula and the sequence of how to rebalance me and resolve the issues. She gave me two exercises to do to resolve any anxiety that might crop up. And she told me that, prior to falling asleep, I needed to instruct my spirit to leave my body through my heart, not my head.

"You're so work- and career-oriented that right now your spirit is leaving your body through your head. That means you're working all night."

That explained a lot. Why I slept restlessly. Why I often woke feeling tense. Why my dreams were often connected to work. Why I ground my teeth and night and had to wear a bite guard.

After my first session with Mary, I decided to try to reconnect with Bakari. It hadn't even occurred to me before to try to talk to him. Especially since my attempt to connect with the tiger at the sanctuary had only worked with the translation abilities from my guides. Nor had I fully realized that Bakari was the catalyst in regard to activating this cellular memory. Now I realized that, in the moment of profound connection with him, he had connected me with my past. I quieted myself and pictured him in my mind. Then I imagined our energy connecting.

"Bakari, did you know that our connection would take me down a path of past-life recall and cleanup? That it triggered my sleep issues?"

I knew it was time for you to come to terms with yourself. I didn't know about the sleep issues. I don't understand that. I have no problems sleeping.

I was surprised that he responded, since my guides had told me that most wild ones wouldn't. But perhaps they were translating for me. Or perhaps Bakari was responding because I'd felt such a connection to him that day.

"Did our connection have any impact on you?"

Forgiveness. I was the cat that took you in the lifetime where you were a safari guide. That's why seeing me triggered your sleep issues. I have no karma for that act. I was simply acting on instinct. But I needed your forgiveness. In that moment, I felt your adoration and awe, and I knew I was forgiven.

"Our connection that day was so profound. The moment our eyes met, I felt a shift. I've thought of you often since then. Have you thought of me since we met?" I asked.

On occasion. But I have resolution.

"If only it could be that easy for me," I said.

His essence faded away, and I reflected on the irony of the situation. Bakari had been a catalyst in my journey to resolve past-life issues that were robbing me of sleep. And I think it's interesting that the word "catalyst" begins with the word "cat," a creature notorious for sleeping eighteen hours a day. While I struggled to get more than six hours. Or the fact that I'd often observed cats, wild or otherwise, lolling in a state of semi-sleep in the most outrageous positions and wished I could sleep like that. Even the saying that cats have nine lives was symbolic for me in this situation. I had nine lifetimes to resolve. So many subtle connections between Bakari and me.

Almost two years after I met him, Bakari contacted me.

I want you to petition for me to be set free.

I responded in confusion. "It isn't possible to set you free. It would be against the law. And they wouldn't even know where to take you. Can you even hunt?"

He scoffed. *You humans are so naïve. Of course, I can hunt.*

"But even if you were free, you'd be hunted and killed. Humans wouldn't stand for a lion to be roaming around. For a predator to be in their midst. And how could you leave the woman who rescued you? I could tell how deeply she loved you. And you her."

I do love her. If she could talk to me the way you can, it would help. But she doesn't know that she can. I need you to go to her and tell her. Then I think I could bear this. I want to talk to her the way I can talk to you.

I told him that I would ask my guides to work with her guides in order to put his request into her mind.

As I was writing his story, I tuned into him once more and asked him if he had a message for the human race.

Stop killing us!

"Do you mean like…canned hunts?"

I mean everything—sport hunting, canned hunts, poaching. Start treating us as equals. You share our planet. You don't own it. You don't own us.

I sat back in my chair, letting his message wash over me. Then I buried my face in my hands and sobbed.

I continued to work with Mary. And I saw subtle improvement. Paula had told me that I would probably always need to take something to fall asleep. And I still do, but drifting off is easier now.

I reflected on the visit with Paula and pulling the three symbolic cards. Lion. Tiger. Bear. And I realized that even the name of the sanctuary had been a catalyst for activating the cellular memory of those lifetimes. Lions, Tigers & Bears. The simple mantra made classic by *The Wizard of Oz*. Sending me on a spiritual quest for balance. For answers. For resolution. And finally, for peace. And all because a noble lion looked my way.

Lions, Tigers & Bears is dedicated to providing a safe haven to abused and abandoned exotic animals while inspiring an educational forum to end the exotic animal trade. Located in Alpine, California, it is a no-kill, no-breed, no-sell rescue and educational facility that allows the animals in the facility's care the opportunity to live out their lives with dignity in a caring and safe environment. For more information, visit www.lionstigersandbears.org.

Prince and Linda

Her life is filled with love stories. A thoughtful and devoted husband of forty-seven years, precious children, and adorable grandbabies. And she lives on an idyllic farm in the south with lush, rolling hills, a sparkling lake, sunflower fields that tower overhead, and tall, sturdy pines that stand like sentinels on the property. Dogs, cats, horses, ducks, geese, and other wildlife all add dimension and beauty to her life. But one special dog will remain in her heart, leaving a void that will be with her forever.

"I've had dogs all my life, but he was my heart dog." Her voice had a charming southern twang.

"What's a heart dog?" I asked.

"One that finds its way into your heart and never leaves."

I met Linda through Facebook in 2011. She'd befriended me after reading my first book, and our lives became intertwined in a casual way. We got to know each other through our daily posts, and I was greatly appreciative of her support of my writing. She was always posting positive messages about my book on its respective Facebook wall, and I felt I had a cheerleader and a guardian angel of sorts in my corner.

She began sharing tidbits about a dog she'd lost. A stout, classic black-and-tan German Shepherd with thick limbs and a sturdy body. His name was Prince, and it had been four years since he'd passed, but his journey to the rainbow bridge still haunted her.

Prince had been with Linda for eleven years. Guarding her. Protecting her. Loving her. They'd purchased him from a reputable breeder as a puppy after their peaceful country home was robbed. They felt the need for more protection. And a German Shepherd seemed the suitable answer.

"Nowadays," she said, "I lean more toward rescuing my animal companions rather than buying them. But back then, I was less aware of the need to rescue. And because we knew the people, respected their reputation, and loved the German Shepherd breed, we chose a male from their recent litter."

Prince proved to be a natural guard dog. At just a year old, his protective instincts were well-formed. If Linda moved, Prince mirrored her, generally leading the way, and looking over his shoulder to make sure she was following him. He came from fine German bloodlines, and the breeder had owned not only the father, but the father's father as well, who were both impressive guard dogs in their own right.

Prince grew up playing with Linda's immense Australian Shepherd, Bear, and he became well known to delivery men, who knew better than to get out of their vehicles if

Linda was out in the yard with Prince. Especially the UPS men, whose open trucks offered little protection from Prince.

"When a delivery man pulled up," she said, "and Prince was in the yard, I'd have to stay inside the house. If I'd ventured into the yard, Prince would have been up in their trucks in a jiffy. But as long as I was inside, Prince wouldn't cross our property line to the road. He was amazing that way, as though instinctively he knew the boundary of our yard. We didn't even have a fence, living in the country the way we did. But he never crossed our property line without me. He was almost *too* protective, even though we'd never trained him to be."

Like many Shepherds, Prince was as gentle as he was protective and spent many hours watching over and herding grandchildren around the house and yard like a four-legged nanny.

"I'd watch that in awe. How he was almost two different dogs. In his presence, I felt completely safe. I never had a doubt how much he loved me. He had such complete devotion to me. I'd never had that connection before."

Prince was six years old when Linda adopted her tiny Chihuahua, and the two bonded quickly. Friends expressed concern when Linda first brought Lucy home, thinking that Prince would be aggressive with the tiny dog and harm her. Instead Prince became Lucy's protector, ensuring that she was safe in and out of the house.

"In the morning, when I'd let them out to relieve themselves, if it was too cold for me to go with them, I'd tell Prince to go with Lucy and watch over her. She was so tiny, she couldn't be out on her own or the hawks might get her. Prince would go out with her and walk side by side until she was ready to come in. He knew exactly what I was asking of him. He was almost human in that respect."

Lucy and Prince formed a deep bond, and although Linda and her husband had other dogs, Lucy hated the others. The only dog she played with was Prince. Their bond was almost as special as the one Prince and Linda shared.

When Prince turned seven, Linda's idyllic world was rocked to the core. A routine mammogram revealed a lump in her breast. When further tests confirmed it was cancerous, Linda began an arduous one-year battle to rid herself of the disease.

Linda told me that when she learned of the cancer, it was a complete shock. She'd had nothing but clear mammograms for years. And the news hit the family right before Christmas.

"You always think that cancer is something that happens to other people," Linda said, "and now it was happening to me. I was scared and shocked, and I kept thinking about my husband, children, grandchildren, and animals. Especially Prince. I wondered how they would make it without me."

Linda underwent a bilateral mastectomy in early January and went home the next day with both breasts gone and a tremendous feeling of loss. But she tried to remain strong and upbeat for her family.

Soon, Linda was able to get out and take short walks again. Prince was always by her side. "I think he knew that something was not quite right with his mama. Because he and my little Lucy saw tears that I couldn't let anyone else in the family see. But his strength gave me strength and the confidence that I could beat this. And he was one of the reasons I had to win this battle," she said.

"Shortly after the mastectomy, I started on a very aggressive chemo treatment that would take two months. It was a horrible process that made me very sick. Joint aches, ulcers in my mouth, chronic digestive issues. But the worst part was the loss of my hair."

Once she completed the first round of chemotherapy, she had a second four-month round of less-aggressive chemotherapy. It left her tired much of the time but was far less invasive than the first round. Once chemo was complete, Linda began thirty radiation treatments, five days a week for six weeks. Radiation left her tired and her immune system compromised. But once radiation was complete, Linda's strength returned. And her hair began growing back. And in a few weeks, she was once again back to play time and daily walks with her Prince.

"He was like a little kid when it was time for our walks since he loved to chase the horses and squirrels. He would only go out a little way from me on our walks, though, and was always looking back to make sure I was there. I loved that about him, and that is why I called him my protector."

Just as Linda was feeling her health return to normal, Prince passed away quite suddenly. His death was a mystery. He had been a perfectly healthy dog in the prime of his life.

"His passing was a shock for me. A deep shock. And completely unexpected. He lay down one day on a walk, and within minutes he was gone. I held him in my arms and wept, begging him through my tears not to leave me. We'd been through so much. He was so instrumental in helping me battle cancer. He was my rock while I was recovering. The one being I felt I could be completely vulnerable with because I wanted to be so strong for my family. It was a tragic loss. After his passing, going for walks was so painful and lonely but also therapeutic in a way because I could still see his footprints on the dirt trail where we walked. It was devastating to me when the first rain of the season washed his prints away and made his death so final."

When Linda first contacted me on Facebook, it had been one year since she'd lost Prince, and my story about losing my beloved Shepherd, Blitz, had struck a chord. And she was a fan of the rescue I supported, often following stories of dogs who had just joined the rescue. Reading about Blitz had reconnected her with her own unresolved grief. And she still mourned for her beloved dog. Her Chihuahua Lucy, her cat Bopper, and her husband's dogs did their best to fill the void, and, although Linda loved them, the hole in her heart wouldn't mend.

"Prince was my baby," she said. "He loved me as much as I loved him. He was such an awesome, wonderful, loyal dog. I grieved his loss for months and going on a year now, but when I think of him, I still just cry."

Finally, when she felt it was the right time to get another dog, her first inclination was not to get another German Shepherd. She felt she might always compare a new dog to Prince. But she loved the breed so much she knew she had to have another. So she rescued a beautiful eight-week-old male sable puppy. A dog she says that turned out to be in many ways the opposite of Prince.

"Rocky has helped me so much to heal from the pain of losing Prince. He's filled that void in my life in some respects. I will never forget my wonderful Prince, and my new baby Rocky does get called Prince quite often, but I am so much happier. But Rocky is a big baby. I love that big, goofy boy, but he is shy, scared of everything, and is no way the protector Prince was. He definitely is just the opposite. He's afraid of everything. But the way he loves to take walks with me and stops to wait for me to catch up just so reminds me of Prince."

"I love that about Shepherds," I said. "The follow-ahead thing they do, always looking back to make sure we're coming. And the reminders one animal companion can provide us in regard to another is simply beautiful. It can be the best healing."

Linda went on to tell me that my ability to talk to animals amazed her. She shared that when she had to travel and be away from them, she sent them special thoughts, hoping to comfort them and telling them she would be home soon. "I never got an answer back from them, but it somehow made me feel better."

One day, long before I had interviewed her to learn about her story, I had a message from Linda via Facebook. She'd been reading my second book and was particularly interested in a story in which I had reached out to a departed dog on behalf of the owner. And it prompted her to ask me if I could connect with Prince. She wanted me to tell him how much she loved him, how tragic his passing had been to her, and how she'd never gotten over his death. She wanted me to tell him that he would always be in her heart.

I promised to respond to her within a week. And when I had enough information, I sent her an email.

Dear Linda,

I spent some time this afternoon reaching out to Prince. My first question for you is, did you get a new dog within a year or two of his passing? It feels like he's back with you.

If not, he might be manifesting his energy via one of the other wild or domestic animals on your property because it feels like he's near you. But he did cross over after he died, so that means he came back. He's telling me that he took the form of a fowl. Those were his words, but I might be jumping to conclusions because I got a sense that he might be one of the ducks on your pond. So grain of salt with that. I don't know if what I'm hearing is accurate. But when you feed the ducks, you might want to pay more attention to see if one in particular seems drawn to you.

When I asked him what he was able to accomplish with you, Prince said two words: freedom and peace. He told me that he is not holding on to anything connected to his death. And he wants you to let go of any guilt you may have. Maybe that's what he meant when he said peace and freedom. Maybe he wants you to be at peace because that will set you free from the memories. If you can be at peace like he is, then you'll have freedom. Maybe that's where he needs you to be in regard to his passing.

He told me he was able to complete something with you...
something in regard to wisdom. Then he showed me a picture
of himself solving a puzzle. I think he thought of himself as a
problem solver, a creative solutions kind of guy. When I tap into
his energy, I almost get a sense that he has a MacGyver type of
energy. That's how he viewed himself.

When I asked him about you, he showed me a picture of
a family at Christmas. That's how he viewed his life with you.
Every day was Christmas. Dreams coming true, magical energy,
anticipation of new gifts, trust in the goodness that will surely
manifest in one's life, and beauty.

Lastly, do you have any creative outlets? I know you're
quite the photographer. Prince wants you to keep pursuing these
outlets. His message for you is that it connects you with your
source of strength and keeps you on your true path rather than
following another person's whims.

Linda responded to me the next day.

Dobie, it was very hard reading this. I cried and trembled,
but I made it through. You just don't know how it touches me,
the thought of you connecting with my Prince. I have tried so
hard to connect with him many times but have failed. After his
passing, my husband told me that he would get me another
German Shepherd, and I said "no" because no other dog could
ever take his place. However, after months of grieving over him,
even though we have other dogs, I finally said, "I am ready for
another German Shepherd." Initially, thought I wanted another
one to look exactly like Prince but then I changed my mind
because I realized that I could never get my Prince back. I chose
a fluffy, sable, male puppy who is nothing like Prince in any way
and named him Rocky. To answer your question, there is an old,

oddball duck that showed up a while back. Not sure where he came from, but he likes it here even though the Mallards do not like him. I will start paying more attention to him and see how that goes. I have recently gotten so interested in photography of the beautiful surroundings on our farm and of course so many amazing sunsets and sunrises. I will definitely have my Angel Boy in mind for sure now as I continue to take pictures. I can't thank you enough for this special gift from my Prince. I will print this off and keep it in a special place forever. Love and God Bless, Linda

When I interviewed her for this story, I asked Linda what she would say to Prince if she could see him once more.

"I'm not sure I would say anything," she said. Then, after a pause, she continued, "It would give me so much comfort to feel Prince's presence again, but I never have. I have a wonderful life and a lot to be thankful for, and I know that. But I still miss him. And I still cry. Every day, I walk through the door and into my home, and I still whisper to him, 'I'm sorry I lost you. And I'll never get over you.' I've always had dogs, but Prince was mine. It was unconditional. I'd never had that. It makes me feel good just to say it. I learned so much about loyalty and devotion from him. He made me aware of the depth of emotion that animals can have. People who haven't experienced this are missing a very special and profound part of life. But if I could see him again, I'd tell him he saved my life. He gave me the courage to get through cancer. I think he knew when I was really well. Because that's when he left me. If I could see him again, I'd just hold him and love on him. And thank him for being the amazing dog that he was."

Sammy and Alissa

"Hurricane Katrina was life-changing for a lot of people," Alissa said. "And I was no different. That hurricane connected me to my calling."

Causing over 1,800 human deaths and devastating wreckage, Katrina, a category five hurricane, was one of the most powerful, costly, and damaging hurricanes to ever hit the Gulf Coast. It rendered thousands of humans and animals homeless.

"I remember seeing an article from Noah's Wish Animal Rescue pleading for volunteers to come help. They'd already rescued 1,900 stranded animals with the hopes of reuniting them with their families. A coworker and I made the split-second decision to go."

The company that Alissa and I work for donated the air miles so they could fly, and other coworkers donated funds for them to take with them. And they used the "Ambassador Hours" that our company gives us each year to volunteer for charity. She had seven days to go there and do what she could to make a difference.

As Alissa continued to tell me her story, I found myself astonished to learn that some people had actually left their animal companions behind, tied in the yard or locked in their homes. It was unfathomable to me that people wouldn't realize they were putting their animals in danger by leaving them. "Luckier" animals were set free to wander the streets and fend for themselves. Each of these scenarios was challenging for the rescue workers and volunteers trying to save them. The fortunate animals they did find alive were brought to a makeshift animal shelter where they were fed, housed, and provided with medical attention until they could be, hopefully, reunited with their families. It was her first experience as both a rescue worker and a witness of a powerful natural disaster.

"I watched the news prior to deploying to New Orleans," Alissa said, "but nothing could have prepared me for the massive destruction I was about to encounter. Cars teetered atop houses. The large stadium had collapsed. Street signs were partially submerged under water. It was like entering a war zone. And something you have to experience to understand."

Once she arrived, Alissa worked twelve-hour shifts feeding animals, walking dogs, cleaning cages, grooming, petting, and comforting these frightened, confused, and orphaned animals. By the third day, her feet were so blistered she had to roll the back of her tennis shoes down so they wouldn't rub her heels. They were hounded by mosquitoes and were constantly grimy and sweaty. Since there was no fresh water, they had to add bleach to disinfect any available water so the animals could drink it. The weather was humid and sticky, and the air was thick. Over 1,000 dogs and cats were crammed in a warehouse. Their chaotic barking reverberated off the metal walls.

I asked her if she felt especially connected to any dog in particular during her time there. She replied that she did have some favorites but that there were many dogs to walk and cages to clean. There wasn't much time to spend with one particular dog.

"But there was one little Chihuahua named Sinker," she said. "He was found in a sink at a home in rising water. The owner had taken her other dogs but left him, probably thinking he would be safe. Sinker really touched my heart. That is one dog I would have wanted to take home and probably the reason I later looked for my own Chihuahua to adopt. Fortunately, Sinker ended up back with his owner."

"Did you see many animals reunited with their families?" I asked.

"Some but not many," she said. "There were still so many people who had not settled back into their homes. I saw more adoptions than reunions. There were several animals that were relinquished because the owners had no way to continue to care for their pets. Many people had nothing left and were forced to move away."

"Besides being able to give back, how did the experience affect you?" I asked.

"As hard as it was," she said, "there was an overwhelming sense of community and love and of giving and gratitude. Local people came to the shelter each day to help walk the dogs and to donate food, supplies, and money. And there were wonderful people who came to adopt animals. Others stopped by just to thank the volunteers. And others came each day to feed and walk their pets while they waited to get back into their homes and reunite with them."

"You said this experience connected you with your life calling. What did you mean by that?" I asked.

"My life has forever changed since this experience. When I returned, I threw myself into animal rescue. It became my mission to help animals. My passion became making a difference for animals. I became a trained animal rescue worker and a certified pet sitter, and I started a side business called Trends For Friends Dog and Kit-Tees With A Purrpose. I created and sold T-shirts to raise money to give back to animal rescue and adoption organizations. Over the years, I've raised several thousand dollars. Rescue is in my blood."

"Are there any rescue stories that are particularly close to your heart?" I asked.

She smiled and said, "They all touch my heart. But Sammy is one rescue I'll never forget."

A work colleague had found two small, lost dogs drinking from a sewer after a massive fire had ravaged the area we live in. Resembling Poodle-Maltese mixes, the dogs were matted, and their white coats were stained with soot. Emaciated at seven pounds each, both dogs were ribby from neglect. One had severe dental issues. His teeth were black and rotten and his mouth crooked from the dental decay.

Alissa's coworker rushed to pick them up and took them to the Escondido Humane Society to see if they were microchipped. They weren't. At the end of the day, Alissa went to the Humane Society to claim them, took them home, and named them Sammy and Sunny. The next day, she reached out to Aussie Rescue, a rescue she worked with, and started networking the dogs.

The vet Aussie rescue worked with inspected the dogs and revealed that Sammy was in worse shape than originally thought. All of his teeth would need to be pulled. And his little body was so riddled with toxins from the infected teeth that the surgery would prove challenging for him. But it was critical that he get the care he needed, so Alissa and Aussie Rescue began to raise funds. Soon they had enough to pay for the procedure, so Sammy was scheduled for the needed dental work.

To complicate matters further, Sunny began to try to dominate her other dogs and was picking fights.

"He'd growl and lunge at my other dogs even though I tried to redirect him. I think he was probably trying to protect Sammy from my dogs. I had discovered at the Humane Society that Sammy was neutered, but Sunny wasn't, which is probably why he was showing aggression toward my dogs. Since I knew they weren't littermates, I decided it would be the best thing for everyone if I rehomed Sunny. And a volunteer from Aussie Rescue adopted Sunny. Right after that, Sammy was scheduled for dental work."

I asked her about the surgery, and she said it had taken hours. They had pulled all but three of his teeth. And his recovery had been both challenging and frightening.

"It was just such a long and complicated surgery for such a little dog. And he'd been neglected for quite a long time, which had compromised his health. I was worried he may not pull through. But he is a survivor and came through it all better and stronger. In fact, after about seven days, he was a different dog."

Within weeks, someone expressed interest in adopting Sammy. But they wanted him as a companion service dog for a terminal cancer patient. And Alissa felt it wasn't a good match. Sammy had been through so much, she couldn't imagine putting him in service to someone he might bond with only to have that person die. Then someone else stepped in, only to have to return him due to allergies.

"When I brought him home, I thought I'd have him for the weekend, not eight months," she chuckled.

Initially, bringing Sammy into the household put some strain on the family dynamics, although in most ways he was a model dog. Quiet and obedient for grooming. Polite and respectful on a leash. And harmoniously integrated with Alissa's other dogs.

Sammy was eventually adopted by a young woman who works with Alissa and me. He accompanies her to work every day and is the mascot for the finance department. He wanders the halls, greeting his mom's coworkers, exploring the different offices, and making sure everyone is present and accounted for. This means Alissa still gets to see him and take him for walks. And when I attend a weekly research meeting in his building, I get to see him too. He touches everyone's hearts.

"To this day, my husband still talks about Sammy with affection and says if Sammy didn't find a home we would have kept him," she said. "I am the one who had to be the voice of reason and remind him five dogs would be way too many."

When I asked Sammy if he had anything he wanted Alissa to know, he thanked her for coming into his life and coming to his aid. After weeks of wandering as a stray, scrounging for food, and being homeless and helpless, a guardian angel had stepped into his life and changed everything. When I asked him what he wished the human race knew about the animal kingdom, he replied that he wished we knew how scary it is to be without a home or a family. I told him that, sadly, there were far too many humans and animals for whom that is a stark reality. His response was that everyone should have a place they call home.

I asked Alissa how her life would have been different had Sammy had never been a part of it.

"Rescuing Sammy was so similar to what I experienced in Louisiana," she said. "There was such a strong sense of community in his situation. So many people at our company, and the Humane Society, and Aussie Rescue rallied around this little guy, and I was a part of that. It was about doing something greater than ourselves. I think that, with each rescue I experience, my heart opens just a little more. It is tragic that there are so many animals in need of rescue, and the thought of not being able to do enough can be overwhelming. I have to remind myself that, even though I can't rescue them all, I can make a difference to the ones that I do."

Alissa went on to say that the beauty in Sammy's story is that he came in as the underdog. The unattractive, unkempt little guy with a mouthful of bad teeth who was completely timid and afraid. But he blossomed into an outgoing adorable baby who parades around the office and has captured every-one's hearts. At one point in his life, he had no one to love him. Now he has all the love he needs.

Turbo and Jayme

Jayme raced down the hall to the veterinary hospital's nurses' station with tears streaming down her cheeks. Choking out the words between sobs, she said, "That dog in the room next to the one my dog and I are in is screaming in pain. I want to pay his medical bills!"

Jayme told me she'd never heard cries like that. She could hear everything the family was saying through the paper-thin walls of the exam room she and her dog waited in. She was distraught, thinking that the dog might not receive the care it needed.

Jayme had rushed her own dog, a plush-coated Golden Retriever named Molly, to the hospital. Allergic to everything, the dog had ingested some leaves from a plum shrub and was heaving and vomiting wildly. Jayme and Molly arrived just as the vet was closing for the evening, so they were referred to the emergency area and ushered to a room. Molly was given medication to remove any remaining bile and then charcoal to absorb the remaining toxins. While they waited, Jayme heard a dog screaming in the room next to them. And the shrill screams gripped her body like a vise and tore at her heart like a saw.

She wrapped her arms around Molly, clutching her to her side. Through the thin walls, she listened tearfully to the muffled conversation. The dog's leg was broken. The people didn't want to put the dog down, but they couldn't afford the vet bill. The vet couldn't legally release the dog back to them without a guarantee of care. Jayme listened in fear, her heart pounding. She felt certain that the people had caused the little dog's injuries, and if they left with him, they would hurt him again.

"That's when I lost it," she said. "I ran out of our room and to the nurses' station. I begged them to let me pay the bills and take the dog. At that moment, the family walked past. A man on crutches, a grandma with a baby, and a woman holding the tiniest black and tan Miniature Pinscher I had ever seen," she said.

The family had agreed that they would relinquish the dog to a rescue. Jayme pleaded with them to let the dog come with her. Instead, the vet took her business card and promised to call her. The family left, without even allowing her to pay to let the dog stay in urgent care overnight.

The next day, the vet called her. The family had relinquished the dog, but by now his condition was dire. "We're losing him," the vet said. "We have to operate to stabilize him. What do you want to do?"

"Here's my credit card number. Do what you need to do to save him," she said.

Jayme had no idea of the extent of the little dog's injuries. At just six months old, he had a badly broken front leg. His carpus, or wrist bone, was fractured, and his ulna, or elbow, was broken in six places. He suffered from broken ribs, a sprained knee, and a severed liver.

His surgery took hours. His leg was so tiny that the surgeons had to use pins instead of screws to anchor the joints in place. To protect the pins, he was entombed in a partial body cast from foot to shoulder, wrapping around his chest. Days later, the tiny pins anchoring his elbow didn't hold, so the entire procedure had to be repeated.

"At first, I had intended to pay for his surgery and find him a home," Jayme said. "But when my family and I went to see him the next day, we were able to hold him and pass him around. He was so happy to be loved and so joyful that I couldn't let him go."

She visited him every day, bringing him toys and a new blanket. His injuries were so traumatic that he spent three weeks in the hospital before Jayme could bring him home. Jayme is an independent medical contractor, and she had just wrapped a huge contract. So she made the decision to take the rest of the year off and nurse the little dog back to health.

Once home, his care required weekly vet checks during which he was anesthetized for a cast and bandage change and X-rayed to gauge improvement. Because of his unstable condition, he had to be immobilized in a tiny crate or held. Since he didn't like the crate, Jayme carried him with her everywhere. Eventually, he was cleared for movement, but even though the body cast should have hindered him, he raced around the house on three legs like a miniature race horse befitting his name, Turbo. His medical care had been very costly, so now he was fast *and* expensive. Jayme changed his name to Turbo Bentley.

Months later, the body cast finally came off, and Turbo was ready to begin a new life.

I asked Jayme how she'd describe Turbo. "Loving, adorable, high energy, spunky, and fearful," she said.

"Why fearful?" I asked.

"Think about what he's been through," she said.

Her description is spot on. I've met him. He's the sweetest little thing, sprightly, and yes, he oozes pure love. I never fail to be amazed at the animal kingdom's resilience. They can suffer so much abuse and neglect. They endure situations that should shatter their trust and harden their hearts, yet most continue to have faith in people. Most continue to love unconditionally. The same can't always be said about the human race.

Turbo was out of the body cast now, but he was still held together by pins, and without the body cast to protect the pins from shifting, he had to be confined to a small playpen where he could have toys. He and Molly played tug of war with a plush toy between the holes of the playpen. Molly always let Turbo win.

"In the beginning, I wondered how Molly would be with him. He was so tiny and fragile that I worried he'd get hurt again. I'd only seen her with one other toy-sized dog. We were in a pet store, and a tiny terrier was in front of us. Molly lay flat on the ground in front of the little dog, never even raising her head. She had an amazing maternal instinct even though she'd never had puppies of her own."

Perhaps because his life was filled with so much pain in the first six months of his life, Turbo became a toy hoarder. As far as he was concerned, all the toys were his. With the exception of Molly's favorite toy. He let her keep that one.

Months later, Turbo had the last of his surgeries to remove the remaining pins. But it would be another six weeks before Molly and Turbo would be allowed to play together. Instead, they took turns in the playpen, watching each other turn the house into a racetrack. When the six-week reprieve was lifted, the two were allowed fifteen-minute, supervised play dates, and finally, thirty-minute chase sessions up and down the carpeted hallway.

At night, Turbo slept in the playpen. When he began to climb out and nuzzle into bed with her, Jayme took it as a sign he was ready to be completely free.

"I wasn't sure at first if I had forgotten to put him in the playpen," she said. "But when I'd put him back in only to wake up with him snuggling with me, I knew he was getting out and that it was time to put the playpen away."

When I tuned into Turbo to ask him about his connection to Jayme, he said that he wanted to thank her for saving his life. He said that she had put him back together body, mind, and soul. Then he showed me a picture of the Goddess Gaia—the caretaker of the planet Earth. She holds Earth in her gentle hands and radiates warmth and nurturing and healing into our planet. Her presence can be felt in the mountains, trees, streams, oceans, and all that is part of our world. To Turbo, Jayme *is* Gaia.

I asked Jayme why she thought she and Turbo had been brought together. She teared up and said, "My dad sent me this dog. Turbo was born five weeks before my dad passed away. When my dad lost his battle with cancer, a part of me died. In the months before Turbo came into my life, I had lost all sense of meaning and purpose. Having Turbo refocused me. I had to pull myself together and take care of this little guy. He needed me. I had to face the things with Turbo that terrified me. With all of his injuries, I didn't know if I had it in me to get through it. I was terrified. Focusing on his healing got me through the biggest loss of my life. Losing my dad was like losing my best friend. Caring for Turbo got me out of my own misery. It allowed me to see beyond my sadness and devote myself to something productive and healing. This little dog pulled me out of my depression. You can't look at him and not smile. He's all heart, that little guy."

In the last few years since I've known her, Jayme has gotten deeply involved in healing animals. It's for this reason that Turbo equates her with Gaia. Her journey to becoming an energy healer is one she calls "accidental yet fated." She was introduced to energy work when she took Turbo to the vet for one of his follow-up sessions. Although Turbo had healed, he still didn't use the once-injured leg much.

She was put in touch with a Reiki worker, who worked with animals to remove blocks and to draw out of their bodies energy that wasn't serving them. After his second visit, Turbo began to use his injured leg and touch the floor with his paw as he raced around the room. The doctor had healed his body, but the energy worker had healed his energy. When Jayme saw the progress that occurred in just two visits, it piqued her curiosity and she enrolled in a few classes. Almost immediately, she felt drawn to work with horses, even though a previous life-threatening riding accident had left her with a deep-rooted fear of the beautiful, but sometimes intimidating, species.

"But I really didn't use what I'd learned much at first, especially with horses," she said. "Eventually, I realized that my fear was stopping me. One day, in meditation, I said, 'OK, God, I'm ready. Where's my horse?' Two weeks later, I rescued my first horse."

Since her first horse arrived, Jayme has immersed herself in learning about the horse from a spiritual, emotional, and physical point of view. She believes, based on the research of experts like Alexander Nevzorov, that horses aren't meant to be ridden and that because of their conformation, putting saddles on their backs and cinching them actually decreases the flow of blood to the muscles that are trying to work, which can have a negative long-term effect on the animal. She shared a passage from his website in which he passionately speaks his mind about equestrian sports:

...*equestrian sport by nature can't be even defined as a sport. Yes, any sport includes records and victories, but these records and victories are gained by one's own sweat and blood, by one's own pains and efforts. And equestrian sport (if we study the issue) represents parasitizing on physical abilities of another living being which may not want to be engaged in this sport but is forced to. So why then do we call it a sport?*

I agree with his thinking and had come to the same conclusion eight years ago and subsequently retired my horse to a life of leisure.

Jayme started her journey by taking classes in equine massage. She then expanded her repertoire to include essential oils, Reiki, crystals, music, and Healing Touch for Animals. She's now a Level Four practitioner in the Healing Touch protocol. It's this passion that prompted her to establish her business, Equine Soul Song, where she uses holistic modalities to balance and heal horses and other animals. One by one, she has been serendipitously drawn to the horses and other animals who needed her.

Long term, her vision is to create an animal sanctuary where her rescued equine companions are able to heal physically and release their emotional and spiritual wounds. When her rescued horses are ready, she is considering developing programs in which humans can come to her sanctuary and learn about leadership from an equine partner and as a result understand themselves more deeply.

For now, she plans to continue her work as a healer so that the animals who need her care are healed on all levels and are able to release their emotional and spiritual burdens. Her current herd includes five rescue horses, two goats, a donkey, two chickens, ten bunnies, my once-foster kitty Willow, a new Australian Shepherd puppy who is Turbo's soulmate, and a newly rescued Chow-Akita mix. So in terms of creating an animal sanctuary, she appears to be well on her way. I asked Jayme if she thought Turbo was the catalyst for the new direction in her life.

"Without a doubt," she responded. "Healing animals is my passion. He opened the door to that, to my life's work. It was because of Turbo's requirements that I looked into and learned other healing modalities. Turbo needed me to learn this so I could help him. And to help him, I had to confront and release my fear. Especially in regard to horses. And now, because of Turbo, I know what my life destiny is. The doctor healed his body. The Reiki worker healed his energy. And I healed his heart." Her voice cracked slightly, and she paused. "He came into my life when I'd lost my beloved dad and my heart was broken and...and I guess...no, I know... he healed me too."

∽ ♡ ∾

For more information on Jayme, visit HealingHarmony@ runbox.com or her Facebook page at Healing Harmony for Animals.

Bear and Dobie

"So is he going to the glue factory today?" Jennifer quipped.

I rolled my eyes and said wearily, "I'm so done with his temper tantrums."

"It's just who he is," she replied.

"I know." I sighed and tossed his halter on top of my grooming kit and pulled up my shirt sleeve to reveal the purple lumps on my shoulder and elbow.

"Ouch. How'd he do that?"

"He kept rearing and striking out while Kirk and I were trying to shoe him. I couldn't control him. And he nailed me."

My horse, Bear, has never been good about getting shoes. He's very clear about communicating that he doesn't enjoy standing still. It's common for him to dance around and fidget. When he gets too antsy, he'll start rearing. But because I rode him, if he didn't have shoes for protection, he'd wear his hooves down too quickly. So not shoeing him wasn't an option.

On one day, he had been particularly bad. As usual, I got to the ranch early so I could work him before Kirk, the shoer, arrived. I let him race around the arena free, and then I lunged him for forty minutes. Then I walked him for about ten minutes to cool him and stretch his muscles. Kirk's truck rolled into the driveway, and he parked and walked toward us with his tools.

"Man, it's a scorcher," he said, commenting on the heat.

"Hopefully, it will work to our advantage and make Bear more manageable."

Kirk bent and began to wrench the nails from the right front shoe with his pliers. Five minutes in, Bear began to get restless, so I circled him and then walked him back to Kirk. Kirk bent and picked up Bear's right front hoof, placing it on a hoof stand to support some of the weight. Then he began to file the hoof to correct the shape and prepare it for the new shoe. Bear arched his neck and bit the air near my sleeve. I jutted my elbow to block him. He does this all the time—the fake biting. It's his way of making a point. His restlessness had progressed to annoyance, and we were only fifteen minutes into the process.

"I *know* you're annoyed," I said. "Everyone who *knows* you is very clear about the fact that you don't like getting shoes."

No response.

I pressed my knuckles into his neck and rubbed in circles on his pressure points, hoping it would relax him.

He shuffled his back feet and then ripped his hoof from the stand, stamping impatiently. Kirk straightened, stretched, and then bent and picked up the hoof again to resume the filing process. Bear shifted his weight and then reared, pawing at the air with his front feet. I jerked his lead line, and he came down with a thud.

"Stop it," I said through clenched teeth.

Kirk ignored it all and picked up Bear's right front foot again, scraping and filing.

Moments later, a fellow boarder walked by with a horse. Bear cranked his head, danced in place, and then snorted, blowing through his nostrils like a dragon.

When they were out of sight, we resumed. Kirk lifted Bear's foot and fit a shoe to the newly trimmed shape. Almost immediately, Bear reared again. He struck out with his front feet and clipped the inside of my elbow on the downbeat. Pain sliced through my arm, and I doubled over. He went up again straight over my head. He came down, smacking my shoulder and trampling Kirk and knocking him to the ground. His right hoof drilled the inside of Kirk's knee, and Kirk balled into a fetal position. Bear reared again, pawing the air with his hooves. Kirk rolled out of the way just as Bear struck the ground. Kirk didn't stand, and he didn't move except to rock, curled in a ball, holding his bent leg. I was in pain and shock, but my mind raced and my brain buzzed with adrenaline. Would Kirk be OK? Could he stand? Was his knee broken? Had Bear crippled him? What if he couldn't work?

Kirk pushed himself up and hopped toward his truck. I held my breath. He walk-hopped until he was hidden from view behind his truck. I could hear him muttering and swearing. In a few seconds, he walked back, limping still. My hand flew to my mouth, and my eyes pooled with tears.

"I am so sorry, Kirk. I don't even know what to say. I wish my reaction time had been quicker. I wish that I could have pulled him off-balance."

"Don't blame yourself. No one can handle him when he's like this. He was like this when I first started shoeing him when he was just five years old. Today...well, this is vintage Bear."

"One of my girlfriends said that Bear is this way because he has my number."

"I'd like to see her try to handle him."

"He *is* a challenge. But I would never forgive myself if he hurt you permanently. When you didn't move...I just... well...my heart stopped."

"No worries. I'll be stiff. But I'm OK. He's done worse things to me."

"Do you want to just stop at the front feet and do the hind another day?"

"Nope. Let's git 'er done."

Kirk lifted the front right, fitted the shoe and tapped the first nail in. The hammer made tinny sounds as it struck the nail. He tapped a second nail. Bear shifted.

"Let go, Kirk! He's going to rear!"

By the time we worked on the left front hoof, Bear was an emotional mess. Continuing to rear and strike out. Once more, Bear broke my grip and reared, but Kirk had already ducked out of range. I jerked on his lead line and backed him up. I'd completely lost my cool. I was angry, Kirk was angry, and Bear was angry. We had become a ticking time bomb. Someone in this triangle needed to be neutral. Karen, a fellow boarder, had been watching in the shadows. I looked her way.

"He's in rare form today," she commented.

"Something's got to give," I said. "I'm so pissed I'm just making matters worse. Would you hold him?"

"Sure. No problem."

Karen has a way with horses. She keeps her cool no matter what. She remains objective and focuses on the task, not the behavior. She remains indifferent to their moods. It's not something I can always do with Bear. I get annoyed with him and expect him to know better. To *be* better. Today, he was an embarrassment. Like an out of control toddler having a tantrum I was powerless to stop. I handed Karen Bear's lead line and walked away.

Kirk worked on the back feet now. Bear couldn't rear with his hind feet engaged. So he stood more cooperatively. I watched from a distance. Bear was calmer but still antsy as he shifted his weight from side to side. Occasionally, he'd rip his hind hoof from Kirk's grip and dance sideways. Karen would calmly maneuver him back into position, and they'd begin again. An hour later, he was done, and Karen handed him back to me. I walked him to his pasture and then re-turned to the barn.

That's when Jen asked me if he was going to the glue factory. And as much as I loved him, I was so done with his behavior.

That night, I had a dream. Legolas and Gandalf, the mythical characters in J.R. Tolkien's *The Lord of the Rings* series, came to me, asking me to travel with them, teach them spiritually, and help them train their horses. It was only a dream.

A day later, I tuned into my guides. "What's going on with Bear and me right now?" I asked. "We are so out of sorts with each other."

Ebb and flow.

It was true. In every relationship, there is an ebb and flow. There are times when you are deeply in love. There are times when you love one another but are not in love. And there are times when you're not even sure you like one another.

Bear and I were in an ebb. I was annoyed with his complexity. I was annoyed with his wildness. I was annoyed with his inability to comply. And he was annoyed with me, although I hadn't a clue what I'd done. I am never abusive, even when I am angry. Nor have I ever been neglectful of his needs. I go out of my way to make sure he has the best of everything.

We'd been such a beautiful team for eleven years. And for most of that time, we'd been the center of each other's universe. Now, I wondered what had happened to us. How could we have been so in love for so many years only to come to a place where annoyance was our new language? Confused, I decided to ask Bear what was going on with him. "Why are you so annoyed with me?" I asked him the next day.

I'm tired of your nagging.

I contemplated his message. He was right. I am always after him to cooperate, behave, and do what I ask. I'm in charge of everything. I try to balance our relationship and to share leadership. I've tried to create a partnership. And for the most part, we *are* partners. But he takes advantage. When you're dealing with a 1,200-pound animal, someone has to be the leader, and it has to be the human. But he's tired of it.

My friend and teacher Jill once told me that he and I have what everyone wants. True love. A true connection. An unconditional love. But in the aftermath of his temper tantrum, I felt none of that between us.

And he doesn't understand the concessions I do make. He doesn't know about the things I do without so that he can have the best of care—chiropractors, massage therapists, energy work, one of the best and most expensive shoers in our area, and top-of-the-line grain and supplements. He doesn't know how hard I've worked to learn to ride him the way he wants to be ridden. I suppose I could tell him, but then I would sound like an ungrateful, overbearing shrew. Or simply a nag.

The next day, as I stood with him in his pasture, I connected with him in hopes of getting to the bottom of our issues. I said, "Bear, we used to be so in love with one another. I don't know what's happened to us. We need to find each other again. Or do we need to let go?"

Bon voyage.

'You're so callous. Such a guy. Why did you come into this life as a horse if you didn't want to do any of this?"

Any of what?

"The whole service thing. Horses are here to be of service."

Who told you that horses were here to be of service?

"People."

Exactly.

"No, I mean sentient people."

What's sentient?

"In tune. Wise. In the know."

What are they in tune with? His tone was sarcastic. If a horse could scoff, he would have. *I repeat, who says I wanted to do any of this?*

"What *do* you want?"

I don't know.

"Well, you need to figure it out."

Why?

"Because I'm done with your attitude."

I'm done with your attitude.

"My attitude? Do you know where you'd be if I hadn't rescued you?"

What makes you think you rescued me?

"You were going to be sold to a jumping barn. You would have been a *commodity*. Traded and passed along. *No one* would have loved you the way I do."

How do you know?

"I just *know*."

How?

"I could see it happening."

Our bickering words ricocheted in my brain like popcorn bouncing off the sides of a hot pan. I sighed. We had become a bitter old married couple. And we were definitely in the ebb.

I took him out of the pasture and let him loose in the arena, watching as he raced around like a madman. The look in his eyes was that of someone possessed by a demon they couldn't exorcise or even run from.

I tuned into my guides. "What's going on with him?"

He's feeling his oats.

"Literally or figuratively?"

There is some sort of chemical reaction happening.

"What is causing it?"

No answer.

Then it dawned on me. I'd changed his supplements several weeks ago. It was a high-quality supplement but not one I'd have put Bear on as a younger horse. It contained more molasses and alfalfa than his previous supplement.

Both ingredients can give him too much energy. I turned my attention back to him and watched him continue to run. He was drenched in sweat now but showed no signs of tiring. Like a kid on a sugar high. Finally, he quieted and walked to me. His head hung low, and his sides heaved. Sweat dripped from him like rain. I made a mental note to switch his supplements.

"You have so much energy. And it is beautiful, but sometimes it's like you disconnect your head and your heart. And you can't think straight. And that's scary for me."

It's scary for me too.

"What can I do to help you with the shoeing process?"

Get out of the way.

"Consider it done. I had planned on paying Karen to hold you from now on. While you're being shod, I mean. It will be better. She's neutral."

Good. You are a catalyst. It's not always helpful. As you said, Karen is a neutralizer.

Suddenly, I understood. Bear and I are the same. High energy. Catalysts. Sometimes, it's a beautiful combination. Sometimes, it's not. Two catalysts operating at odds are combustible.

I had never considered this before. That someone who is neutral can be a neutralizer and that someone who is a catalyst can sometimes bring too much energy to the table. And I realized that we must always consider the energy we carry with us and how it affects those around us.

Now I knew that I was the cause of his behavior. I was co-creating his meltdowns. I expected the worst, and he gave it to me. I keyed up. He keyed up. And we fed off each other's energy. It was a powerful epiphany. But I was chagrined. For eleven years, I'd been blaming him for something I'd unknowingly played a part in.

"I'm so sorry, Bear. I had no idea, but I should have."

It's not completely your fault. I am a handful. And you should know that your energy is beautiful too.

He lowered his head and touched the back of my hand with his velvety nose. My heart swelled, and I could feel a warm band of energy surging between us as our hearts reconnected. And just like that, we were out of the ebb and back into the flow.

In the weeks that followed, I made the decision to re-tire Bear. I came to the realization that he was done with the structure of our dressage training. He was done with doing things my way, and he was ready to be free. The next time Kirk came to the ranch, we removed Bear's shoes. For good.

About the Author

Dobie Houson is an activist for animal rights, an animal communicator, and the author of *Finding Forever: The Dogs of Coastal German Shepherd Rescue* and *Four-Legged Wisdom: Sacred Stories from an Animal Communicator.*

An ardent activist for animal rescue, Houson is founder and executive director of Finding Forever, a foundation dedicated to raising money and awareness for animal rescue causes through the arts.

A lifelong animal lover, she has worked with dogs, cats, and horses. But it was her desire to understand and connect with animals on a deeper, more meaningful level that ultimately led her to study animal communication, including honing her telepathic skills. She has trained with some of the country's most respected intuitive counselors and animal communicators and, today, is a sought-after teacher and trainer herself.

A professional communicator and prolific writer, Houson contributed to *Why We Ride: Women Writers on the Horses in Their Lives*, a popular anthology edited by writer and literary agent Verna Dreisbach. Houson also heads StrategiCreation, a marketing and communications consultancy for business start-ups.

When she's not working with animals, Houson serves as director of marketing research for The Ken Blanchard Companies, a global consulting firm specializing in leadership and talent development. Her research has been published in many world-class academic journals.

She lives in Valley Center, California, north of San Diego, with her family, her animal companions and her lively horse, Bear.

Finding Forever—A Passionate Foundation for an Important Cause

Finding Forever was formed to raise money and awareness for animal rescue causes through the arts.

Founded in 2011 by author and animal communicator Dobie Houson, Finding Forever has already raised thousands of dollars for animal rescue groups, sanctuaries, and charities. Among them: Coastal German Shepherd Rescue, Hearts United for Animals, Best Friends Animal Society, Alley Cats Allies, Fur and Feather Animal Sanctuary, and USA Battle Buddies, a non-profit organization providing service dogs to wounded veterans. A portion of the sales from Houson's books are donated to the foundation.

The Humane Society estimates that U.S. animal shelters care for 6-8 million dogs and cats every year, and that approximately 3-4 million of them—many being young, healthy, and adoptable—are euthanized.

Finding Forever is committed to finding solutions.

Made in the USA
Coppell, TX
04 July 2022